Beside the Seaside

D1386711

For my wife Jenny, my travelling partner
through history and through life.

Beside the Seaside

*A History of
Yorkshire's Seaside Resorts*

John Heywood

PEN & SWORD
HISTORY

First published in Great Britain in 2017 by
PEN AND SWORD HISTORY
an imprint of
Pen and Sword Books Ltd
47 Church Street
Barnsley
South Yorkshire S70 2AS

ISBN 978 1 52670 464 1

Printed and bound in India
by Replika Press Pvt. Ltd.

Typeset in Times New Roman by
CHIC GRAPHICS

Pen & Sword Books Ltd incorporates the imprints of Pen & Sword
Archaeology, Atlas, Aviation, Battleground, Discovery,
Family History, History, Maritime, Military, Naval, Politics, Railways,
Select, Social History, Transport, True Crime, Claymore Press,
Frontline Books, Leo Cooper, Praetorian Press, Remember When,
Seaforth Publishing and Wharncliffe.

For a complete list of Pen and Sword titles please contact
Pen and Sword Books Limited
47 Church Street, Barnsley, South Yorkshire, S70 2AS, England
E-mail: enquiries@pen-and-sword.co.uk
Website: www.pen-and-sword.co.uk

Contents

Acknowledgements

Like all books that delve back into the past, this look at the growth of Yorkshire's east coast resorts is built upon the countless hours of research and study of authors and historians past and present. To them, and to all those who left their writings and diaries for the use of others, often several centuries later, a great big thank you. Those contemporary accounts, together with newspaper articles from the time, throw so much light on our ancestor's thoughts and concerns, their likes and dislikes and how, just like many of us, they enjoyed time spent by the sea. I am also extremely appreciative of those people who answered my call for their memories of holidays spent on the Yorkshire coast over the last sixty years.

I would like to add special thank you to the all those employees at Wakefield Library's Local Studies Centre who have been patient and efficient during the many hours I have spent there. I am also grateful for the work of the staff at the East Riding and North Riding Archives together with Scarborough and Bridlington Libraries.

Love and thanks are due as always to my wife Jenny, who has proofread and edited this book and just as importantly stood by me when I have been totally obsessed with its completion. Now that it is concluded and spring will soon be upon us, we can't wait to spend more time back by the sea.

Introduction

Writing about Bridlington in the *Yorkshire Weekly Post* of 11 September 1915, an unknown journalist penned these words. They could have been about any of the county's resorts and sum up perfectly what it means to be beside the seaside. Moreover, the sentiments expressed could have been those of visitors at any time over the last three hundred years:

> 'People are always to be found on the sands, in the tiers of promenades, on the Princes Parade, on the new Spa, in the streets shopping, flirting, boating, reading, sewing, knitting, reprimanding the children, listening to the pierrots, writing postcards, giving the eye that gladdeneth, puffing the expensive holiday variety cigar, sipping cups of coffee and other sips and sups, listening to the band, tapping toes to keep time, humming airs and cracking jokes, giving backchat of the most frivolous pertness, admiring the neat ankle, delighting in the grace of some unknown divinity, comparing apartments and landladies, criticising or praising their culinary capabilities, commenting on style, and how some people follow the fashion at all costs, sneering at the ultra stylist or at those lacking it or aping it, or openly buying fashion of a later date than Victorian, bathing walking, cycling, tennising, golfing, fishing.'

Yorkshire's coast continues to attract visitors in large numbers. It stretches between two of the great rivers of the north, and forms more than one hundred miles of the most varied scenery in the country, much of it still relatively unspoilt.

Yorkshire's northernmost boundary is the Tees, the gateway to the third largest port in the United Kingdom and the petrochemical,

Flamborough, North Landing. (US Library of Congress)

chemical and steelworks of Middlesbrough. But once you turn your back on this smoke-filled landscape, rural England prevails until the coast meets the Humber Estuary at Spurn Point. Although it is peaceful now the beauty hides, in some cases, an industrial past where ironstone and alum were mined, quarried and shipped in large amounts.

Around one half of the coast is rugged, with limestone cliffs towering above the sea where rocky inlets and sandy beaches punctuate their majesty. Where access from the sea was possible, fishing villages grew up. Access from the land was often difficult and these frequently became the domains of smugglers. Runswick, Staithes and Robin Hood's Bay are prime examples and whilst tourism has inevitably led to changes, they remain today much the same as they were.

In some of these places, the beaches were broad and sweeping and the villages developed readily into resorts. Saltburn, Whitby and Scarborough grew quickly when railways started to bring visitors to the sea. Scarborough, proud of its claim to be the oldest seaside resort in the country was originally a spa town and is still the largest and most prosperous of these developments. It is beautifully situated over two bays with its former medieval royal fortress rising above them. Whitby, with its evocative ruined abbey, atmospheric old town and a picturesque harbour, has been a magnet for artists and writers for over one hundred years.

The attractive town of Filey has welcomed visitors, including royalty, since the eighteenth century, attracting those seeking the peace and quiet that its neighbours could not offer. For many years though,

Robin Hood's Bay (US Library of Congress)

Staithes (US Library of Congress)

the town was synonymous with the Butlin's Holiday Camp which brought prosperity to the area until its closure in 1984.

The geology changes again after Filey and the white chalk cliffs of the Yorkshire Wolds are seen at Bempton, Speeton and Flamborough. Much of this section of the coast is a mecca for seabirds of many kinds and attracts nature lovers

The Wolds turn inland at this point leaving the rich farming country of Holderness; sadly, it is also one of the most vulnerable in the world and in parts is retreating at one to two metres per year due to coastal erosion. Sheltered below the cliffs of Flamborough is the family resort of Bridlington.

From this point, the sands run almost unbroken to Spurn Point, incorporating the small resorts of Skipsea, Hornsea and Withernsea, popular in the past with those seeking an escape from the mighty port of Hull and the River Humber.

INTRODUCTION

The coast stirs our imagination and inspires us to dream. It allows us a freedom that we often find nowhere else. No wonder then, that over the last three hundred and fifty years, generations and generations have sought health, happiness, good company, entertainment fun and relaxation on its shores. How did this love affair with the Yorkshire coast start? How did it develop? This book seeks to take you on a journey through its past and discover what it really meant to be 'Beside the Seaside.'

Modern day Scarborough, a view that has changed little over the last two centuries (Adobe Images)

Taking the Waters
1620–1931

In his *Tour thro' the Whole Island of Great Britain,* the writer and traveller Daniel Defoe wrote of Scarborough:

> 'The town is well built, populous and pleasant, and we found a great deal of good company here drinking the waters, who came not only from all the north of England, but even from Scotland. It is hard to describe the taste of the waters; they are apparently tinged with a collection of mineral salts, as of vitriol, allom, iron and perhaps sulphur and taste evidently of the allom.'

The story though had begun some 100 years earlier in the late 1620s, when Mrs Thomasin Farrer, the wife of former Scarborough Bailiff and local worthy John Farrer, discovered spring waters emanating from the base of the cliff, to the south of the town. The rocks that had been in contact with the water were stained a reddish-brown colour. Upon sipping the liquid, it was found to have a slightly bitter taste. Believing that the water may contain medicinal properties, she bravely experimented on herself before persuading family and friends to do likewise. Word of the water's healing properties soon spread around the area.

There were in fact two springs which she named the North and South Wells, the north being of chalybeate water (a mineral spring containing salts of iron) whilst the south contained more saline and was believed to be of a purgative nature.

The 1640s and '50s were far from the ideal time to be visiting Scarborough to take the waters, however, as it found itself embroiled in the English Civil War (1642–1651). In 1645, the royalist forces at the castle were subjected to a five-month siege, one of the bloodiest of the entire war. A further siege followed in 1648. Following the end of the conflict, over ten years of puritan rule followed significantly affecting the number of visitors arriving at the Spa.

It has been said that if it was Thomasin who discovered the springs, it was 'Robert Wittie who was responsible for bringing them to the attention of the nation'. Wittie was born in 1613, the son of a former Mayor of Beverley, He was a Doctor of Medicine having studied at King's College, Cambridge before returning to Hull, first to teach and then to practice as a physician in the town. He moved to York sometime prior to 1665, from where it is known that he had been sending some of his patients to Scarborough as part of their treatment. He was to become the Spaw's (as it was called) new champion.

In 1660, Dr Wittie, in the first edition of his book, *Scarborough Spaw – or A Description of the Nature and Vertues of the Spaw at Scarborough in Yorkshire,* claimed that the waters were a cure for all manner of disorders from 'wind to leprosy'. He followed up his publication with a revised edition in 1667 in which he now claimed that the waters were a successful treatment for 'apoplexy, catalepsie, epilepsie and vertigo' together with diseases of the nerves, asthma, scurvy, jaundice and many other ills. Wittie recommended that they should be drunk mid-May to mid-September, when the waters had not been diluted by the winter rain.

Even with the limited medical knowledge of the period, it was not at all surprising that some of Wittie's claims should have been disputed by his colleagues. Whether this was jealousy, a preference for inland spa towns such as Harrogate and Knaresborough, or a genuine belief that his assertions were nothing more than unproven rantings is a matter of conjecture. One of his main adversaries was Dr William Simpson of Wakefield, who published his response in his book *Hydrologia Chymica* in 1669. Whilst accepting some of the properties of the waters, he, in marked contrast to Dr Wittie's beliefs, espoused a regime of physical exercise, fresh air and good food as being far more likely to cure illness than spa water.

Wittie also promoted the benefits of sea bathing as a cure for the same range of complaints. A few years later, when a couple who had previously been unable to conceive a child found that the wife became pregnant after bathing in the sea off Scarborough, its fame was assured. Within just a few years the town was to be transformed from a popular spa town to the first English seaside resort.

That was most definitely not the case in 1697 when early adventurer, Celia Fiennes came riding into town. Although she acknowledged that 'Scarborough was a very pretty sea-port,' her description of the Spa suggests that it was still undeveloped and that visitors had to struggle across the sand twice a day to partake of the waters. It did not yet suggest that the town would become a bustling hive of activity in the years to come.

The only routes to the springs were either a dangerous descent from the cliffs or across the sands, as outlined by Miss Fiennes. There were no buildings to shelter those taking the waters and they were open to whatever elements the North Sea (or German Sea as it was then known) might throw at them.

The corporation who owned the spa began charging a small amount for large quantities of water in 1684. Having previously undertaken no improvement work at all, they eventually inserted a large cistern to collect and store the water. The local authority made several more enhancements, including making the spring secure and ensuring that at high tides the well-head would be covered, thereby preventing contamination from the seawater.

Perhaps the most important change and the one that showed that corporation was taking the Spaw seriously, was in 1700 when they inserted a tenant, Richard Dickinson, known by all it would seem, as 'Dicky,' the self-proclaimed 'Governor of Scarborough Spaw'.

Dickinson unfortunately suffered from several deformities. In his book of 1819, James Caulfield described him:

'as one of those beings whom nature, in her sporting moods, formed and sent into the world to prove the great variety of her works, though he had every limb and member in common with

DICKY DICKINSON,
Governour of Scarborough Spaw.

SAMOS unenvy'd boasts her Æsop gone
And FRANCE may glory in her late Scarron.
While ENGLAND has a Living Dickinson.

1725

Richard (Dicky) Dickinson – the self-styled governor of Scarborough Spaw
(Wellcome Trust)

other men; they were, however, so strangely contrived and put together, as to render him the universal object of admiration and laughter.'

He continued that Dickinson possessed humour:

'in a most eminent degree, this joined to the singularity of his figure, contributed to bring him into great notice among the gentry and others who visited Scarborough Spa.'

What really set Dickinson apart, however, was that he had a vision of what was needed to attract and, more importantly, retain wealthy visitors to the Spa. He wasted no time in constructing three buildings, two conveniences, one for the 'Ladeys' and 'Another house for the Gents' together with a larger structure known as 'Dicky's House'.

John Feltham, writing in 1803 outlined the original layout:

'The Spa lay on the sands fronting the sea to the east under a large cliff the top of which is above the high water level 54 yards. The staith or wharf projecting before the spa house was a large body of stone bound by timbers, and was a fence against the sea for the protection of the house. It was 76 feet long and in weight, by computation, 2463 tons. The house and buildings were on a level with the staith.'

Whilst there is no doubt that by 1720 Dicky had made the Spaw a resounding success, it was not appreciated by everyone who visited. Sarah, Duchess of Marlborough who visited in July/August 1732 found it 'very dirty and expresses vast poverty in every part of it'. She also complained about the difficulty in accessing the wells, a problem that wasn't to be fully solved for many years 'it is besides so extremely steep to get to either in a coach or chair (sedan), that I resolve to go no more'.

In 1727, the cost of spa water had risen to one shilling per anker (forty litres), and when bottled and sold locally, sixpence per dozen. Much of the profits went to the town bailiffs. Such was the success of

Thomas Gent's view of Scarborough published in 1735. It shows the Spa prior to the landslip. (North Yorkshire Council County Council)

the Spa, that when Dickinson's lease came up for renewal in 1734, the rent was raised from one to forty pounds per annum. He himself charged five shillings for men and two shillings for women for the use of the facilities.

A Gentleman from London, writing to his friend in 1733, likened Scarborough to Montpellier and confirmed that the town had 'been frequented by all the principal Nobility and Gentry from all parts of the Kingdom; its reputation increasing in proportion as tis more known'. Of those visitors during the season, two were dukes, seven had the title earl and two of baron.

Dickinson's good work and the fortunes of the town of Scarborough were to be almost overturned when on 28 December 1737 and in the twenty-four hours following, the Spa House, its building, the well and the staith were all engulfed in thousands of tons of earth. The events were described dramatically by John Feltham:

'On Wednesday, December 28, in the morning, a great crack was heard from cellar of the spa-house; and, upon search the cellar was fond rent [a hole], but at that time no father [sic] notice was taken of it … and on Thursday between two and three a third crack when the top of the cliff above it rent two and twenty-four yards in length and thirty-six in breadth and was all in motion slowly descending and so continued until dark. The ground thus rent, contained about an acre of pasture land and had cattle feeding on it.'

The land 'had sunk nearly seventeen yards perpendicular'. Dicky and his wife Peggy were lucky to escape with their lives, losing their home and possessions. The events had obviously taken a great toll on him and just six weeks later, he was dead.

Scarborough responded to the tragedy with great resolve and no little action. Contemporary reports state that within two days of Dickinson's death, men with horse drawn carts were digging out where the Spa had been. The corporation was fully aware of the importance of the spa to the town and its development and had in a very short time found the spring water under the rubble, and indeed, some accounts spoke of two new springs being discovered.

The authorities were also quick to pronounce that the water was now even better than before the landslide. Whilst this is highly unlikely to have been anything more than good publicity, it was backed by Charles Cotterill, a surgeon and Dr Peter Shaw, a local physician.

In its 17 May edition, the *London Daily Post* announced that a 'Room for the Reception of the Ladies had been completed'. It was a brick building with a chimney at each end and measured fifty-three feet by twenty-six feet and was thirteen feet high. An equivalent room for the gentlemen would be ready just ten days later. An engraving, *The South Prospect of Scarborough in the County of York*, published in 1745, appears to show that there was in fact just one building with two separate entrances. The wells and the building were protected to some degree from the sea by a two-tiered wall topped with wooden rails.

Following the death of Dicky Dickinson, Captain William Tymperton, formerly master of Wills Coffee House in London, was appointed the new governor of the Spaw. The new appointee, however, was an employee of the corporation rather than a tenant, on a salary of twenty guineas per annum. Noticeably, there was no house as part of the contract.

In the publication, *The History and Antiquities of Scarborough,* Thomas Hinderwell made a special note of one of the later governors of the Spa, William Allinson. He was remarkable for 'his longevity, having lived to the age of 103 years, in the possession of all his faculties'. Hinderwell continued that Mr Allinson had 'always lived well and that the spaw-water was his sovereign recipe'.

The period following the rebuilding of the spa facilities and completion of a carriageway down to the beach were to be its most financially successful, with sales of bottled water reaching a peak in 1738-9, before dropping off steadily but significantly from that date. The reduction in the number of visitors taking the spa water also steadily declined but at a slower pace. By the mid-1780s, the number of visitors paying for the season at the spa had fallen by half, to just over three hundred. Part of the reason for the decline was the lack of investment, both in improving access to the Spa and in providing facilities and attractions such as gardens and walks in the neighbouring area. A sophisticated and wealthy clientele demanded and expected more.

Not to be outdone, the small town of Filey also claimed health giving properties for its spring water, which was situated to the north of Carr Naze (at the landward end of Filey Brigg). John Cole, writing in 1822, suggested that the spa water had been known of for over one hundred and fifty years. It was very hard to access being at the edge of a cliff. In the 1870s, there was a dispute over rights of access to the spa and the source of the spring water was eventually boarded up. Despite attempts to resurrect the spa in 1951, coastal erosion had now taken its course and the source of the water collapsed into the sea.

Whitby was another town where plans to rival Scarborough as a spa town came to nothing. A poem of 1718 by Samuel Jones told the story of the recovery from jaundice of Customs Officer Andrew Long after taking the spa water at Whitby. There were in fact three sources of water, one on the shore by the West Cliff which was destroyed by the sea. Another was by the East Pier, also now long gone. The only surviving spring was the Victoria/Bagdale Spa Well House, hidden at the rear of Broomfield Terrace and enclosed in a round Victorian building. The problem that Whitby encountered in its bid to become both a spa and bathing resort was its remoteness. This was not to be addressed until after the coming of the railways in the mid-nineteenth century.

Scarborough's neighbour and later seaside rival, Bridlington, announced that an 'incomparable new spaw' had been discovered just south of the town and by 1738, the spa waters had been advertised. In his short book, *Picturesque Excursions from Bridlington Quay*, John Furby referred to two springs, the first, situated by the harbour, was 'the striking phenomena of an ebbing and flowing spring of fine fresh water'. This was discovered in 1811. Piping had been inserted to keep the spring open. The spring water was used mainly for laundry and was 'used in the washing of the finest linen'. William White, writing in 1840, claimed that a reservoir had been constructed to store the water and the volume of water could 'supply the whole navy of England'.

The second spring was situated about a quarter of mile to the north west of the Quay and issuing from a pleasant garden was a chalybeate spring of similar medicinal properties to the ones in Scarborough and Cheltenham. Any success, however, was to be short lived and by the time visitors had started to visit Bridlington in great numbers, the heyday of taking the waters was over.

Times were indeed changing though and sea bathing and the entertainment that a resort offered were becoming more important than the taking of the waters. Writing in 1769 during his visit to Scarborough, Thomas Pennant complained that:

'This [the Spa] and the great conveniency of sea-bathing, occasion a vast resort of company during summer it is at that time a place of great gayety, for with numbers health is the pretence, but dissipation the end.'

The early nineteenth century saw a series of near disasters. The Spaw House was damaged by a storm in 1808, and a very high tide in 1825 saw the Spa almost washed away. *The York Chronical* reported that the tides marked 'their progress with desolation to vessels' and that part of the Spa was 'dilapidated in a deplorable manner'. Fortunately, the corporation responded swiftly, undertaking the necessary repairs and rebuilding work within a very short period of time.

Without a doubt, the major achievement in this period was the construction of the Cliff Bridge. For the first time in two hundred years this was to provide visitors to the spa with a safe and accessible route avoiding both perilous descents, muddy and flooded paths or long walks across the sand. The Scarborough Cliff Bridge Company was formed in November 1826, with the aim of creating an iron bridge spanning the valley from St Nicholas' Cliff to the Spa. It was to be some 414 feet long and tower 70 feet above the valley below. Scarborough corporation granted the Company a lease for 99 years at five shillings a year for the land covered by the bridge and a new footpath from its southern end to the spa. The following year, the Corporation granted the Company a lease of the same length on the Spa itself. It was also at this time that 'w' was removed from the word 'spaw'.

In the reprint of his history of Scarborough, Hinderwell confirmed that the foundation stone was laid on 29 November 1826 and that 'in less than eight months the beautiful structure was finished'. The 19 July 1827 was fixed as the date of the opening of the bridge to the public. The same publication gave a first-hand account of the events of the day:

'At an early hour, multitudes from the surrounding country crowded into the town and long before the appointed time for the ceremony, the Terrace and the opposite cliff presented a sight at once impressive and richly diversified. A procession which had formed at the Town Hall at 10, was of the most respectable kind, consisting not only of the company, but also of many distinguished visitors … The day was unusually fine,

The Cliff Bridge with the tollbooths still in operation. The bridge brought about a safe and convenient route to the Spa.

the sky was unclouded and scarcely a breeze played on the bosom of the mighty ocean.'

Other reports spoke of a brass band playing rousing and patriotic music and of a plethora of speeches. A dinner for eighty was held at five o'clock at Donner's Long Room which was 'sumptuous and elegant'. The day was an important milestone in the history of Scarborough and its development as a seaside resort.

Fees for the use of the bridge were settled at five shillings for a yearly ticket and three shillings for one valid for a fortnight. The spring water continued to be free for local residents. The bridge was a great success, but even this did not appeal to the delicate sensibilities of some. Augustus Granville writing in 1841 remarked that:

'as I paced cautiously at first this airy structure, I could hardly look down to the far-removed strand below, through the slender planked pavement, perforated with apertures for the escape of rainwater, without a recoil of the blood, a dizziness and a feeling of horror.'

A sign of the way the Spa's future was to develop was when an orchestra appeared for the first time in the 1830s. Gradually, the Spa was to become one of the most popular entertainment venues outside London. During this period, however, the building continued to be rocked by a series of disasters, often just after building work had been undertaken.

A severe storm in February 1836 devastated the Spa, resulting in a complete rebuild. The new Gothic Saloon was opened in 1839 and included a concert hall seating five hundred, a garden, promenade and an outdoor area where orchestras would perform. *Theakston's Guide* of 1840 described the new building as 'being in the castellated style, and is much admired for its chaste and elegant appearance'. The opening of the building was celebrated by a 'public breakfast and was attended by most of the fashionable visitors then in town and by many of the respectable inhabitants'.

The Spa's new 'Gothic Saloon' opened in 1839. (Wellcome Trust)

Granville did not seem enamoured either by the building or by the spa waters. He did concede that they were effective in the treatment of the newly named complaint of 'heartburn'. Given the high level of magnesium sulphate in the water, this was hardly surprising.

By the time the Gothic Saloon had opened, there were already calls that the building was too small. Additions were made in 1845 including a saloon and ladies room amongst others. The spa waters were now of a secondary concern with music, dancing and refreshments being the priority. As a result, Sir Joseph Paxton, the famous landscape gardener and architect, of Chatsworth House and the Crystal Palace fame, was employed to redesign the building. Paxton's plans included extending the promenade and the building of a new music hall behind it. Additional plans included a covered bandstand and a three-storey observation tower. The original saloon was to be retained as a refreshment room. He also suggested improving the grounds, including balustraded stone staircases and stone flowerbeds behind the new buildings. Work started on the new spa in 1857 and on 20 July 1858, the new Spa Hall opened with a grand concert. The new hall and its galleries was capable of seating two thousand people. This was followed by the improvement to the gardens and the building of the Prospect Tower. In 1871, eight additional acres of land to the south of the Spa were also purchased.

The year 1875 saw further work carried out to protect and restore the wells. The major change that year though was the opening of the Cliff Lift, linking the Spa with the Esplanade. When it opened on the 6 July it was the first cliff railway in England. The opening day saw 1400 passengers paying one penny each to use the new lift.

The Spa thrived following the many improvements but once again tragedy was just around the corner and on 8 September 1876, parts of the Spa were gutted by fire. After much intense debate amongst the members of the committee of the Company, the Music Hall was swiftly replaced by a larger hall designed by architects Verity and Hall. The new building was opened in 1880 by the Lord Mayor of London, accompanied by the Lord Mayors of York, Scarborough and others

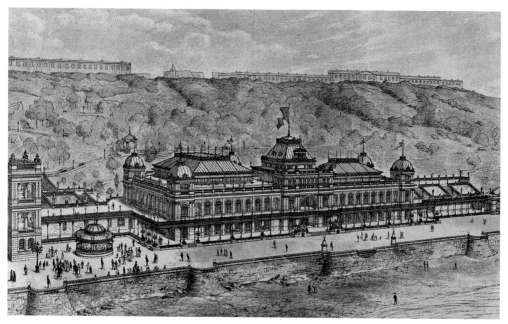

The Spa following the Verity and Hall additions. (Wellcome Trust)

from the surrounding provincial towns. *Bulmer's Directory* of 1890 enthused over the new work:

> 'A stranger arriving on the broad promenade is struck with the grand pile of buildings before him, erected on the sight of the old saloon, and which comprise the Grand Hall, theatre, picture gallery, restaurant etc. and built at a cost of £70,000 … The decorations of the Grand Hall, the Spa Theatre and Refreshment Buffet are of the most elaborate design.'

The directory did not forget the springs and included the most recent analysis of the water's content.

Over the next one hundred years, changes and improvements to the Spa occurred on a regular basis. Very few of them, however, were connected to the spring waters. By 1914, the South Well had closed and in 1931 the North Pump Room was buried beneath a new stall selling ice cream and drinks. Whilst the days of taking the waters were over at Scarborough, the Spa in its many guises has continued to entertain and amuse the town's visitors up to the present day.

As a footnote it is interesting to observe that whilst Bridlington's flirtation with becoming a spa town was limited to a few years in the early to mid-nineteenth century, the town did eventually erect spa buildings of its own, but more of that later!

A Dip in the Sea
1667–1911

In the second edition of his *Scarborough Spaw* book published in 1667, Robert Wittie claimed that apart from taking the spa waters by mouth, sufferers from gout should also bathe in the sea. Such bathing could also 'kill all manner of worms' and was also capable of 'drying up superfluous humours and preserving from putrefaction'. In his view, the only place in England to purify the body with water both internally and externally, was Scarborough.

Whilst Wittie's claims, were as usual, completely exaggerated and based on little scientific evidence, they were also going against all medical and social practices of the time. There appeared to be a general aversion to immersing oneself into water altogether during the sixteenth and seventeenth centuries. The population very rarely washed, let alone bathed. It is not surprising therefore, that Wittie's recommendations were not immediately followed by any great number of people.

Whilst some bathing in the warm mineral rich waters of Bath and Buxton was undertaken, plunging the body into the freezing temperatures of the German Sea was another thing altogether. Amongst the wealthy and privileged, swimming and bathing in the sea (and even in rivers and lakes) was considered vulgar, immoral and the preserve of sailors and the lower classes.

There is no doubt, however that by 1730, the wealthy clientele that Scarborough encouraged had begun to change their minds. In a *Journey from London to Scarborough* in 1733, the unknown writer confirmed:

'It is the custom, for not only the Gentleman, but the Ladies also, to bath in the sea; The Gentlemen go out a little way to

16

sea in boats (call'd here Cobbles) and jump in naked directly; tis useful for Gentlemen to hire one of their boats a little way to sea. The Ladies have the Convenience of Gowns and Guides.'

The sight of those 'ladies' had an effect on at least one gentleman who was driven to verse, comparing the bathers to Venus:

'Yes Sure: Why not! Since here you see
Nymphs full as beautiful as she,
Emerging daily from the sea.'

An engraving, *Perspective Draft*, by John Setterington from 1735 is important, as it shows bathers in the sea off Scarborough Spaw. The image reveals bathers, mostly naked, swimming from boats whilst others are bathing from a wheeled hut at the edge of the water. This is thought to be the earliest image of a bathing machine in the world. It is not known whether the machine was operated by Dicky Dickinson, Governor of the Spaw.

There is no doubt that Scarborough was well in advance of the southern resorts of Brighton, Weymouth and Margate, whose advancements after 1750 were brought about by the writings of Richard Russell of Lewes in Sussex, amongst others. He was again a man of dubious medical credentials, promoting the health benefits of sea bathing together with the drinking of sea water. Amongst his more outlandish suggestions was that:

'a little draught of seawater is convenient immediately upon coming out of the sea because by purging the belly it prevents the blood flying to the head.'

His description of the perfect sea bathing resort, however, almost fitted Scarborough to a tee and cannot have harmed its reputation. 'Clean and neat,' the sea to be 'highly loaded with sea salt,' the shore to be 'sandy and flat for the convenience of going into the sea in a bathing chariot' and surrounded by 'lively cliffs and downs'. The combination of sea bathing and the renowned spaw helped to make Scarborough the first seaside resort. Writing some years later, John Cole reminded his readers of William Hutton's comments of the benefits 'that the drinking of these waters and, bathing, effected upon his daughter'.

By 1787, there were twenty-six bathing machines operating on the sands. At that time, the cost of using the facilities was one shilling plus tips. By the end of the century, there were over forty machines operating. There are several wonderful descriptions of the bathing machines but by far my favourite is from the novel *The Expedition of Humphrey Clinker* written by Tobias Smollett in 1811:

'Imagine to yourself a small, snug, wooden chamber, fixed on wheel-carriage, having a door at each end, and upon each side, a little window above, a bench below. The bather ascending into the apartment by wooden steps, shuts himself in and begins to undress.; while the attendant yokes a horse to the end near the sea, and drawers the carriage forwards till the surface of the water is on a level with the floor of the dressing room; then he moves and fixes the horse to the other end – The person within being stripped, opens the door to the seaward, where he finds the guide ready, and plunges headlong into the water. After having bathed, he re-ascends into the apartment, by the steps which had been shifted for that purpose and puts on his clothes at leisure, whilst the carriage is drawn back again upon the dry land; so that he has nothing further to do, but open the door, and come out as he went up; should he be so weak or ill as to require a servant to put off and on his clothes, there is room enough in the apartment for half a dozen people. The guides who attend the ladies in the water, are of their own sex; and they the female bathers have a dress of flannel for the sea; nay, they are provided with other conveniences for the support of decorum. A certain number of the machines are fitted with tilts, that project from the seaward ends of them, so as to screen the bathers from the view of all persons whatsoever.'

Bathing Machines at Bridlington from George Walker's Costume of Yorkshire *(1814). A nervous bather emerges from the machine whilst a naked swimmer watches on.*

Down the coast, at Bridlington (or Burlington) Quay, the town was suffering; both the port and its trade, import and export, were in decline. Attempts to become a spa town to match Scarborough had also fizzled away to nothing.

In the summer of 1765 an advertisement was placed in the *York Courant* Newspaper. stating that:

'complaint having been made for some time for the want of conveniences at Bridlington for bathing and of the roughness of the shore on the North Sands; this is to acquaint gentlemen and ladies who require sea bathing that commodious houses drawn by horses, and all other accommodations as at Scarborough are now completed and ready for their reception, and a convenient road made for carriages to go down to the

South Sands, which are as firm and free from stones as any sands in England.'

By 1767, accommodation was being advertised as suitable lodgings for the bathing season. The town was beginning to attract the gentry from around the East Riding of Yorkshire and by the end of the century, the number of visitors had increased significantly. A former previously regular visitor to Scarborough, John Courtney of Beverley, went as far as to say that in his middle age he now preferred Bridlington and stayed frequently in the town with his family.

The first guide book to Bridlington appeared in 1805 and was entitled *A Description of Burlington Key*. Written in verse, it made the following short reference to sea bathing:

> 'Sea-water bathing, hot or cold,
> Revives the health of young and old.'

George Walker's illustration *Bathing Machines at Bridlington* from his 1814 publication *The Costume of Yorkshire,* shows a bather alighting from one of the machines on the town's North Bay.

Even smaller resorts benefited. *Theakston's Guide* of 1840 confirmed that 'Filey's sands are by far the best on the east coast' and for those who enjoyed sea bathing 'every possible accommodation in the use of sea bathing machines' was available. Writing in 1869, Dr Oliver stated:

> 'Redcar … 6 miles of sands … how well is adapted to the debilitated class of invalids not only by reason of its powerfully tonic atmosphere and excellent bathing but because of the natural facilities afforded by its extensive beach for easy exercise and locomotion.'

It is also known that Hornsea introduced bathing machines around the start of the nineteenth century.

In tandem with the rise in popularity of sea bathing, was the opening of hot and cold seawater baths. Attracting those who could

In latter years, bathers were often surrounded by machines as they waded into the water. (US Library of Congress)

not or would not bathe in the open sea, their popularity rose. By 1798, there were two such establishments in Scarborough and by 1840 this had risen to five.

The first to open was operated by Wilson and Travis, two local surgeons. It was soon to be known as just Travis' Baths. Writing in his *History and Antiquities of Scarborough*, Hinderwell described the baths as:

> 'Situated at the entrance to the cliff and was originally opened in 1798. In 1822 it was rebuilt and the interior fitted up with every attention to comfort and elegance. The baths are of wood and marble, and are adapted for either plunging, sitting or the recumbent position. They are supplied every tide with the purest sea water, and admit of every variety of temperature. Rooms are also fitted up for steam, vapour and shower baths.'

The author continued to depict the other baths:

Weddell's Baths

'These baths, situated near the pier, were erected in 1812, and are supplied with the purest water, fresh pumped from the sea between the piers, at a part remote from all contamination. They are neatly fitted up with all the requisite accommodation for warm, cold and shower baths.'

Harland's Bath's

'Are situated in what is called the New Road at the bottom of Vernon Place. The situation combines as much as possible, privacy with convenience. One of the baths has been fitted up for bathing in a sitting position. Contiguous to the original building is a little structure containing a plunge bath; intended chiefly for those, who for various causes, are prevented from bathing in the sea. These baths are constantly supplied with the purest sea-water.'

Champley's Baths

'These are situated in Mr Cockerill's garden, nearly central between the Cliff and Brunswick Terrace. They are quite of modern structure, and have a commanding situation. They possess all the accommodation of the others, and what some may conceive an additional advantage, one suite of rooms for ladies and another for gentlemen.'

Vickerman's Baths

'These baths were erected in 1829, and adjoin the Marine House, situated on the beach. From their contiguity to the sea they are readily supplied with water, and possess similar accommodations to the other.'

In 1825, the price of the baths would have been around two shillings and sixpence for a warm bath with an additional sixpence going to the attendant; a Shower Bath, one shilling and sixpence and sixpence to the attendant. At these prices, the baths were very much the domain of the upper classes.

By the early 1860s, the baths in Scarborough were facing harder times. What had once been Harland's Baths was now the sanatorium. Champley's and Weddell's had disappeared. Public baths were opened under Bland's Cliff. These were aimed at a very different market. Prices were lower with visitors being able to swim in warm seawater for just sixpence. Personal bathing cost one shilling. Opening hours were from six in the morning until ten at night. The baths closed in 1931 and the building (with the first floor removed) became Corrigan's amusement arcade.

It is perhaps appropriate at this point to also mention the General Sea Bathing Infirmary. Opened in 1804 on Foreshore Road, it was based on a successful, similar hospital in Margate. Amongst the diseases treated by a regime of bathing and fresh air was scrofula (tuberculosis). Thalasso-therapy (the seawater cure) had originally been propounded by Richard Russell. Such treatment had been the preserve of the wealthy and it was hoped that the new Infirmary would expand the benefits to the less privileged.

In 1852, the Infirmary was extended, incorporating two adjacent buildings taking the total number of beds to twenty-four. Eight years later, however, it had outgrown even this extension and a completely new building was placed on its site. The *Bulmer's Guide* stated that the new Infirmary had admirable internal arrangements and 'would accommodate patients with bed board and the best medical advice'.

The first hot and cold baths were opened in Bridlington by Benjamin Milnes in 1803. The baths were provided in:

'rooms replete with conveniences, built beneath the terrace, which supply the invalid or the timid with the advantage of sea bathing without the necessity of plunging into the open sea.'

In 1815, new baths were opened on Cliff Terrace, with separate suites for men and women. The next facilities to open, some thirty years later, were Bishops Improved Baths on the Esplanade. They only lasted until about 1860 when they were demolished during building of the new sea wall parade.

After a lengthy period when the only available facilities were those on Cliff Terrace, George William Travis in July 1874 opened his new baths to some considerable fanfare. The *Bridlington Free Press* dated 4 July reported that:

'On the upper floor which is in fact on a level with the road are Ladies' Baths which comprise Turkish, Russian or Vapour and hot and cold salt or fresh water Baths. Each bathroom is fitted with everything appropriate. Descending to the floor beneath are Gentleman's Baths arranged in much the same manner and equally convenient and comfortable.'

The sea baths were certainly beginning to move away from their original purpose and resembling more the spas we know today. Healthy? Yes. But also a place to relax and unwind.

Travis's Baths were still going strong in 1888, but under new

An advertisement for George Travis' New Baths opened in 1874.

ownership and were now known as Pool's Baths. It also had a Steam Laundry attached. A swimming pool was part of the attraction. Under various owners it survived until bomb damage in the Second World War caused its closure. Bridlington was sadly left without indoor swimming facilities until 1987.

The first sea water baths in Whitby, inventively named the 'The Sea Bathing Establishment' came into existence prior to 1828, although the facilities left something to be desired. For the price of one shilling the bather was given a tin bath to use which would be filled with jugs of seawater from the harbour, after which he or she climbed in and bathed. Even then, one had to be properly and modestly dressed from below the knee to the neckline.

Two events were to have major changes on the resorts. The first was the dawn of the Victorian era, where morals and values were in

POOL'S BATHS,

Queen's Square and North Pier,

BRIDLINGTON QUAY.

Open daily from 6-30 a.m. to 9 p.m.   Sundays from 7 a.m. to Noon

PURE SEA WATER,

Direct from the Sea every Tide.

SEPARATE SUITE OF BATH ROOMS FOR LADIES.

Hot or Cold, Salt or Fresh Water Bath, 1s. each, Six for 6s.

LARGE TEPID SEA WATER SWIMMING BATH,

6d. each, (Boys under 14 years, 3d).   Water kept at 65 degrees.

**Turkish Bath, 2s., Ten Tickets, 15s.
Medicated Baths, 2s. 6d. each**

POOL'S
STEAM LAUNDRY

QUEEN'S SQUARE, BRIDLINGTON QUAY.

All Kinds of Laundry Work Promptly Attended to.

GENTLEMEN'S FLANNELS

Washed, Dried, Pressed, and ready for delivery in Four Hours.

TROUSERS, 6D. ; SHIRTS, 3D. EACH.

GENT'S SUITS CLEANED FROM 2s. EACH.
WHITE CURTAINS CLEANED

At 10d. per Pair; and returned iu Four Days.

By 1888 Travis' Baths had become Pool's Baths and featured a steam laundry.

marked contrast to those of the Georgian/Regency period that had just ended. The second was the introduction of the railways, which brought a completely new type of visitor to the coast.

Whilst historians Peter Gay and Michael Mason argue that the modern view of Victorian prudery can be over-exaggerated and that, despite the use of bathing machines, it was still possible to see people bathing in the nude. A change from the medicinal immersion into the sea water to swimming and going into the sea 'for fun' did lead to outcries from some members of the population.

Throughout most of the eighteenth and into the first half of the nineteenth century, sea bathing in Scarborough had continued in much the same manner. Men, women and children mixed together on the beach at the southern end of the South Bay. Whilst most people changed in the bathing machines and a proportion of men did bathe naked, there were no recorded complaints prior to 1840.

In 1847, complaints were made against the bathing methods that were in operation decrying them as 'in defiance of all decency'. The objections led to the council banning male bathers on one small section of the beach, a fudge that pleased no-one. More complaints followed, including one from a father of a large group of girls aged from ten to eighteen, who with the utmost zeal, protested that 'every physical attribute was unblushingly exhibited and perfectly distinguishable from the windows of houses, the promenade and the beach'. Whether he had a telescope at the window is unclear! The outcome was that by 1852, new bye-laws had been passed stating that boats should not go within fifty yards of a bathing machine, men's drawers or women's gowns had to be worn between the hours of 7am and 9pm by all except boys under the age of twelve.

Even stricter measures were introduced in 1861 when the first 'Indecent Bathing' Bye-law was introduced. All bathers were now required to change in a bathing machine and no one above the age of 12 was allowed to bathe naked on any beach. Separate areas were set aside for men's and women's machines This was followed by an amendment in 1867 that echoes some modern day laws, where the onus was placed on the bathing machine operators to ensure that all the bathers were decently covered. The rules, however would appear to have been frequently broken. New tougher restrictions imposed in both 1882 and 1892 threatened bathers with fines.

The charges were prohibitively expensive for many and as such paddling was the most that the less well-off visitor, especially those visiting for the day, could achieve. Certainly, in Scarborough's case there was an initial reluctance to encourage the 'Day Tripper' and to continue catering for the wealthy and middle classes. Latterly, the council did try and address the matter to some extent by placing a maximum charge of sixpence for the use of bathing machines, including the use of towels. There was certainly an air of the South Bay being the exclusive end of the town and the north catering for the rest.

The restrictions placed on bathers were introduced throughout all the resorts on Yorkshire's east coast. As late as 1901, Withernsea introduced new stricter byelaws for:

'fixing the stands of bathing machines on the seashore and the limits within which persons of each sex shall be set down for bathing; and within which persons shall bathe'.

The new laws strictly segregated male and female sea bathing in all but one area of the beach. It was the council's aim to keep at least one hundred yards between the sexes. The regulations also laid down minimum standards of dress:

'Every person of the female sex who may hire or use any bathing machine for the purpose of bathing, or may be set down from such a machine for such person, shall, at all times whilst bathing, wear a suitable gown or other sufficient dress or covering to prevent indecent exposure of the person.'

A similar ruling related to male bathers. Interestingly, the fees for the use of a bathing machine were still capped at sixpence with an additional sixpence being sought for the use of an attendant. The fines for breaches of the byelaws had, however, risen to five pounds.

At the same time, the nearby resort of Bridlington was leading the way in opening up mixed bathing areas. Segregation had become a deterrent to families. Travis Elborough wrote:

'Democratised by the railways, the seaside, once the terrain of adult entertainments, was becoming more about ... the family.'

Although the new areas demanded that bathing costumes covering the neck to knee were worn, it was the beginning of the end for the bathing machine as bathing tents gradually replaced them.

By 1904, even Scarborough, with its reluctance to offend the wealthy and middle classes upon whom it had depended for so long, realised that the world had changed. It provided bathing tents beyond the Spa on the South Bay and on the North Bay sands. Even in the early twentieth century, the resort proved it was still at the forefront of innovation. Wooden beach/bathing huts had first appeared in

Another first for Scarborough – Linked Beach Huts (Adobe Images)

Bournemouth in 1910. The pioneering decision to link a row of them on the North Bay in 1911 was Scarborough's own, and this example was quickly followed by three more rows on the South Bay.

In describing the beach huts, this comment from Historic England sums up perfectly the wider transformations that were taking place at seaside resorts all along Yorkshire's east coast:

> 'The concept of beach huts reflect changing ideas about social decorum; getting changed for bathing in a hut at the top of a beach and walking into the sea in full view was rather a liberated activity.'

Bathing at the seaside had changed forever and paved the way for the twentieth century and the gradual transformation into the way we use the resorts to this day.

Did You Know? –
Seaside Bathing Fashions

It is hard to separate the history of the bathing costume from that of the rise of the seaside resorts. Prior to the late seventeenth century, there were no real bathing costumes at all. The first bathing wear was based on what women were wearing in the waters at Bath and other inland spas. Celia Fiennes writing in 1687 described their dress as such:

> 'The ladies go into the bath with garments made of a fine yellow canvas, which is stiff and made large with great sleeves like a parson's gown; the water fills it up so that it is borne off, so that your shape is not seen, it does not cling close as other linen which looks sadly in the poorer sort that go in their own linen.'

She then continued to describe the gentlemen as wearing: 'drawers and waistcoats of the same sort of canvas, this is the best linen'. In the eighteenth century, whilst many men and boys continued to bathe naked, the vast majority of women wore the shapeless bathing gowns, a long, loose-fitting shift made with a high neck and full sleeves. The hems were sometimes sewn with weights to avoid the embarrassment of dresses floating up above their knees. The gowns were fashioned either from stout linen or, more usually, from woollen flannel, recommended for extra warmth and protection in the chilly sea! They were neither stylish nor practical. Women were also careful not to expose themselves to the sun. A tan was exclusively the preserve of the farm worker and manual labourer. Ladies sought to keep their skin pale and pure, a beautiful asset.

Fashions altered very slowly and it wasn't until the mid-nineteenth century that real changes were seen. Bathing costumes became more stylish and even to the daring two-piece suit, consisting of a gown covering the body from the shoulder to the knees, teamed with 'Turkish' pants, trousers that were gathered in at the ankle and resembled those worn by women in the middle east. The style was pioneered by Amelia Bloomer, forever remembered in the name given to this style. During the Victorian era modesty prevailed, although towards the end of the period, with the bloomers rising to knee length and full sleeves shortened, the tide was turning. The tunics were also becoming shorter and more fashionable often with sailor style collars.

(US Library of Congress)

Men's bathing suits were by now of leotard design with a chest section. To bare the chest was considered immodest. The suits were fitted with sleeves and were knee length. They were coloured black or striped to prevent them being mistaken for underwear. By the end of the century, mixed bathing was becoming acceptable. To walk across the beach from changing tents in a swimming costume gradually became the norm.

In 1907, controversy arose when Australian swimmer, Annette Kellerman (the first woman to swim the English Channel) was arrested for indecency in Boston, USA, for wearing a close fitting one piece suit. Eventually, the swimwear she championed became acceptable for

(US Library of Congress)

competitive swimming and paved the way for the swimsuits we recognise today.

Whilst some women still preferred two piece swimsuits, even these began to change. In the early years of the twentieth century, necklines got lower and shorts replaced the bloomers. The costumes also became more figure hugging as new fabrics were introduced. By the late 1920s, sun tans were seen as a sign of good health and available leisure time and not as the preserve of the manual worker. Swimsuits became far less restrictive, cut away at the thigh like shorts, often with little over skirts to hide the thighs. The suits also incorporated cut away sections around the midriff. It was not until the mid-1930s that it became more acceptable for men to bare their chests on the beach and to wear short legged trunks.

It was in 1949 that the new sensation, the bikini, was launched. Named after Bikini Atoll in the Pacific, the two-piece costume completely bared the midriff for the first time. Many women remained loyal to the one-piece suit. The corseted suits with bra tops featured in so many glamorous Hollywood films, ensured the popularity of the 'one piece,' alongside the striking new bikinis.

Board and Lodgings
1665–1900

It was all very well having a spa of excellent repute, together with some of the best bathing waters in England, but if there was nowhere suitable for the noble and wealthy visitor to stay when they came, Scarborough's growth as a seaside resort was going to be short lived.

By the year 1665, there were three types of accommodation available – inns, lodging in private houses or renting a house. According to his autobiography, Henry Newcome, a non-conformist preacher and activist at the Collegiate Church of Manchester, had arrived with his wife in June of that year. They had intended to stay at an inn but they found upon their arrival that it was full. They found lodgings in the home of a Mr Hickson. 'Two neat rooms we had and the woman of the house was mighty respective of us.' The preacher was extremely pleased that they had saved fourpence per day and that they could dine alone, or as he put it 'we were free from mixed company'.

The couple were back the next summer, where once again they found their intended inn already full. On their journey, they were offered a room in the summer home of a Mrs Dickinson, which was not initially accepted. The reason for this would appear to have been that their hostess had spent a substantial amount of time in London, which at the time was ravaged by the plague. A meeting with Dr Wittie put their minds at rest and the thrifty preacher this time saved 'a third part of the charge it would have cost us at the inn'.

The redoubtable, Celia Fiennes, on her quest to ride side-saddle through every county in England, found that there was limited accommodation in the town and that the best 'were in Quakers hands, they entertain all people, some in private houses'.

A few years later in 1732, our old friend, Sarah, Duchess of Marlborough, writing to her granddaughter, found her accommodation as noisy and dirty as she had the Spa and the town. She continued to complain that:

> 'after I am in bed every night, I am awaking with the barkings and howlings of dogs and hounds which is kept all around me for the entertainment of fine gentlemen in this place'.

As someone more familiar with the comforts of Blenheim Palace, this is hardly surprising.

In *A Journey from London to Scarborough in Several Letters from A Gentleman*, the writer remained very tight lipped about the quality of the accommodation, but did comment on the food available in the town:

> 'There are several ordinaries in the town, the principal of which are the New Inn, the New Globe, the Blacksmith's Arms and the Crown and Sceptre. The company dine commonly about two, and have ten or a dozen dishes, one of which is generally rabbits, which you have here in the utmost perfection; their mutton is, I think, at least equal to Barnstead Downs [part of the South Downs near Epsom], and the nearness of this town to the sea supplies them with plenty of fish at very reasonable rates, and for poultry, they have a here a poulterer, who finds it worth his while coming from London every summer. Persons of all ranks, gentlemen and ladies together sit down without distinction, each paying their club, which is one shilling; after which, they collect round the company for wine etc. which is generally one shilling more.'

Arthur Rowntree also added that it was usual to drink a glass of Spaw-Water with the meal.

Scarborough had been as slow to understand that good accommodation was as vital to its success as it had been to realise the commercial benefits of the Spa itself. Changes began to take place in

This view of Scarborough in 1780 shows the town beginning to develop.

the 1760s, when the new buildings on the west side of St Nicholas Cliff were erected. Adding to Scarborough's list of firsts, it is arguable that these were the first purpose-built seaside lodgings in Britain. The terraced houses could accommodate three to four families in each, together with their servants. Behind the houses was stabling for several horses and garaging for carriages. The area itself eventually became popular for promenading in the evening.

By 1785 when Schofield's *Guide to Scarborough* first appeared, the 'New Town' with Newborough, Long Room Street, Harding's Walk (now Huntriss Row) and Queen Street had begun to be developed. Some of the building were again purpose built for visitors. In his book, Schofield enthuses over the new developments. Newborough is a 'Great and handsome street,' whilst Queen Street 'would not discredit a metropolis'. Nearby was Long Room Street which was given over to visitors and contained the two public assembly rooms, Newstead's and Donner's and some of the largest lodging houses in the town.

In 1791, the Reverend Doctor James Falconer applied to build a new road into the valley, with an easier descent to the beach from which carts and waggons were excluded. The new road opened up space for new development and made the area an even more attractive space for visitors to the town and spa. Further development in this area followed, including Vernon Place and Brunswick Terrace.

With the new buildings came higher prices. Schofield quoted ten shillings per week with servants' quarters at half price., towels and sheets included, although the visitors were responsible for their washing. A kitchen with all utensils was twenty shillings and a servants' hall, ten shillings. Many of the visitors ate an ordinary at one of the inns.

Just a few years later, rooms could fetch far more. On the heels of these price increases, new boarding houses slowly began to appear. It was to one of these that William Hutton retreated with his daughter in 1803:

'The accommodation we found were of three sorts; to take a furnished house, if a family arrived, which may be done from six to ten guineas a week; or, take apartments in a family, and find food and servants yourself; or board and lodge in a family at a stated price. We chose the last. The terms were twenty-five shillings each, for my daughter and me, exclusive of tea and liquor, and ten shillings each for a bed. The servant half or seventeen shillings and sixpence, and the same sum for the horse, including corn.'

The other alternative were the inns. These were often tied in with the coaches that delivered the visitors to their destination. Perhaps the most well-known was the Bell Inn, which had the best view of them all. It was also renowned for its breakfasts where 'an ample supply of rolls, accompanied lavish quantities of ham and local shrimps'. Amongst the other inns were the Bull, opposite the end of Huntriss

Row, which was renowned for the size of the stabling available and was advertised as a gentle and commodious inn, furnished in a genteel manner. Other inns included the Beverley Arms, in Newborough, the London Inn and the Talbot.

By 1811, there were over 120 houses given over to accommodation for visitors, the majority of which were still lodging houses although several boarding houses were listed. Many of the proprietors were also involved in other business ventures, as the extract from the *Scarborough Guide* of that year shows.

LIST OF LODGING AND BOARDING HOUSES
NEWBOROUGH STREET

Mr Rudsdale, Grocer

Mr W Wilson, Music Shop

Mr Tortle, Breeches Maker

Mr Todd, Toy Man

Mr Broadrick, Bookseller

Mr Willis, Surgeon

Mr Dobson, Factor

Mr Tesseyman, Stay-Maker

Mr Mallory, Grocer

Mr Cullen, Draper

Mr Smith, Draper

Mr Frankland, Saddler

Mr Cass, Grocer

Mr Newton, Baker

Mr Estill, Draper

Mrs Clark, Milliner

Mrs Mitchell, Grocer

Mssrs Marflitts, Drapers

Mr Bancroft, Watchmaker

Mr Harrison, Tea Dealer

Mr Bye, Brazier

Mr Harland, Druggist

Mr Lord, Ironmonger

Mr Powley, Taylor

Mrs Hall, Draper

Mr Dale, Brazier

Mr Welch, Draper

Mr Barton, Breeches Maker

Mr Percy, Shoemaker

Mr Windle, Grocer

Mr Tomlinson, Shoemaker

Mrs Brown

Mr Stephens, Ironmonger

Mr Thirwell, Druggist

Mrs Duesbery

Mr Anderson, Saddler

Mr Cockerill

Mr Watkinson, Grocer

Mr William Smith

Mrs Fox

Mr Bulmer, Taylor

Mrs Cooper

The growth in the new town led to calls that the area should have its own place of worship that would accommodate many of the summer visitors, alleviating the pressure on the Parish Church. Public subscriptions met some of the cost and Christ Church in Vernon Place opened in August 1828.

Further development of the New Town came in the period 1835 to 1850 with the construction of Belvoir Terrace and the Crescent above Ramsdale Valley to the south west of Brunswick Terrace. Around the spa area, the Esplanade was built which afforded almost every building being given over to visitor accommodation of one sort or another. Several large villas were built opposite the crescent of terraced houses, one of which eventually became the summer residence of Lord Londesborough.

Visiting in 1839, Augustus Granville was very complimentary about the accommodation on offer and especially the food. Granville, who was staying at the Bell was particularly happy with the breakfasts, where not just 'excellent tea, tea cakes, muffins and new laid eggs' were served but also 'cold beef and raised pies, and shrimps and potted and marinaded fish of many kinds'. He continued that such food was to be found at many inns in the town.

The visitor, whilst finding lodging houses and separate houses quite expensive, especially during the season (1 July–12 October), discovered that boarding houses were very good value with rooms and bed, including four meals a day, available for between for four shillings and sixpence to six shillings and sixpence per day.

Scarborough had arrived at a turning point. It was the eve of the coming of the railways, an event that was to change the lives of the seaside resorts for forever. In nearby Bridlington (Quay), the resort had been growing since the late 1760s, when the town had started to capitalise on the new fashion for sea bathing.

In 1767, William Standish bought two properties and was soon advertising them as accommodation for the bathing season. Bridlington appealed to the local gentry from the East and North Ridings of Yorkshire, who found it quieter than its neighbour Scarborough. As a later visitor was to note 'Bridlington attracts

41

An elegant Scarborough crescent, one of many similar streets built in the town mainly for the use of visitors. (Adobe Images)

numbers of that class of visitor for whom Hornsea is too quiet and Scarborough too gay'. By the time *Baines Directory* was published in 1823, the Quay possessed some seventy five lodging houses and twelve inns and small hotels.

It was at such a lodging house that Charlotte Brontë stayed in September 1839 with her friend, Ellen Nussey. It was her first visit to the coast. After staying for three weeks with a Mr and Mrs Hudson just outside the town, the friends moved to a house on Garrison Street, possibly run by Ann Booth who is listed in *Pigots Directory* of 1841. The cost of staying in such an establishment was more than their limited budget would allow. They found:

> 'that at the end of the week when bills were asked for … they discovered that moderate appetites and modest demands for attention were of no avail as regards the demands made upon their small finances.'

They had, however, thoroughly enjoyed the time away on their own, the 'realisation of enjoyment had been as intense as anticipation had depicted'.

Prior to 1850, most of the accommodation was on the Promenade and a few of the surrounding streets mainly King, Queen and Prince Street as well as the aforementioned Garrison Street. Many of these properties had originally been wealthy merchants' houses before being taken over for the use of Bridlington's growing number of visitors. In 1868, architect Joseph Earnshaw was brought in from Derbyshire to oversee further developments in the town including the Crescent, Marlborough Terrace and Tennyson Avenue. Much of this accommodation was for the use of visitors.

By the 1880's, the Hilderthorpe area of the town had begun to develop with two thirds of the properties on Bow Street and Ferndale Terrace being occupied by lodging house keepers. Some of the best lodging houses were to be found near the railway.

The resort town of Filey is a product of the Victorian era, having previously being a small agricultural and fishing village of around one hundred houses. At the time of *Pigots Directory* of 1834, accommodation was in one of the five inns – the Britannia on Queen Street, run by William Anderson, the Hope (Church Street), the Packhorse (also on Queen Street) and the Ship. The fifth, the New Inn (later the Hotel) was owned by Thomas Foord and was possibly the first purpose built visitor accommodation in the town. It also served as the posting house, where horses were kept for post riders or for hire to travellers. Although not listed in Pigot's there were many rooms available for rent in the homes of local residents. These were often the dwellings of fishermen, keen to supplement their meagre incomes. However, visitors were beginning to visit Filey in increasing numbers, the directory confirming that:

'the village is resorted to in the season by numerous families, who are attracted hither by the grand scenery around, and the remarkably fine sands; and for the accommodation of visitors.'

Perhaps, the most important development in the rise of Filey as a resort was the work of John Wilkes Unett, a Birmingham solicitor, who, in 1835 instructed architect Charles Edge to create the New Filey Estate. It extended south west from Queen Street and included the sea front, west of the Ravine. The crowning glory of the new resort was The Crescent, stretching for about one quarter of a mile, 'the tall white houses' surrounding the Royal Crescent Hotel which was placed at its very centre. Whilst the majority of the work was completed during the 1840's, later additions were made until 1881. Filey now attracted the aristocracy and the wealthy both from this country and beyond. King Leopold II of the Belgians visited in 1873 and was followed by Prince Alfred, the Duke of Edinburgh in 1880 and Prince Albert Victor in 1890.

A view from the sea shows the New Filey Estate with the beautiful buildings on the Crescent. (Adobe Images)

Charlotte Brontë was a faithful visitor to the town. Following the death of her sister Anne in 1849, she moved from Scarborough with her friend, Ellen Nussy, and lodged at Cliff House with Mrs Smith. She returned on her own three years later and noted the growth in the resort:

'I am in our old lodgings at Mrs Smiths; not, however in the same rooms, but in less expensive apartments. They seemed glad to see me, remembered you and me very well, and, seemingly, great good will. The daughter who used to wait on us is just married. Filey seems to me much altered; more lodging houses - some of them very handsome – have been built; the sea has all its old grandeur.'

Of the four main resorts, Whitby was perhaps the slowest to develop. As Andrew White put it, 'Until the nineteenth century Whitby's charms were almost unknown to the outside world'. The real motivating factor in Whitby's transformation into a resort was the coming of the railways. Whilst the vogues of taking spa water and sea bathing had only a very minor effect in the town, the new breed of visitors arriving by train most certainly created the longed-for popularity and success. The market that Whitby was aiming for was most definitely the upper middle class with clergy, military and successful businessman all to be seen as part of the new wave of visitors.

The development of accommodation suitable for visitors was almost all on the West Cliff. Where in the past a handful of inns had sufficed, many of the new buildings were erected especially for their needs. Hotels and large houses, suitable for either boarding or letting out for the season were built. Whilst George Hudson, the 'Railway King' is often credited with the idea for the work he in fact, would appear to have built on the proposals of the Whitby Building Company, which had been around for some years. It is beyond doubt, however, that it was Hudson who moved the project forward at some speed. East Crescent and East Terrace including the Royal and Kirby hotels together with the eastern half of the Royal Crescent and the Esplanade, were all completed by 1858. Sadly, the western half of the Royal Crescent was never finished.

From Whitby's East Cliff, Hudson's new West Cliff developments are clearly shown nicely in this 1890s image. (US Library of Congress)

To speed up the construction process, a small railway was added to carry building materials up the cliff. Following the end of the work the railway was turned into a road. Both carried the name The Khyber Pass.

Esk Terrace was a new development near the railway station, It was followed by a succession of rows of boarding houses, some more aesthetically pleasing than others. Although further developments were planned on the West Cliff, much of the work was never completed and as such, even with all this progress, it is easy to overstate the importance of tourism to Whitby in the latter half of the nineteenth century.

Holidays with pay and even the Bank Holiday Act of 1871 were still some years off when the railways first came to the east coast. Whitby had realised that it was not the miner and the mill worker but the wealthy and the burgeoning upper middle classes that the locomotives initially brought to the sea. Hotels were opened at all the resorts to cater for their expanding and demanding needs.

One of the first hotels to be built in Scarborough, was the Crown. It took its place on the Esplanade when there was very little else there. In anticipation of the opening of a railway line between York and Scarborough, architect John Gibson laid the foundations of the hotel before handing the construction of the hotel to the South Cliff Building Company.

When John Fairgay Sharpin visited the town in 1845, he was taken with both the newly completed building and the area in general. He was to become its first tenant. On 1 June 1845, *The Times* contained an advert advising of the opening of the new establishment:

The West Cliff today. (Adobe Images)

'J.F. Sharpin respectfully informs the Nobility and Gentry that he has entered upon the above new anti extensive Establishment, which he is having fitted up in a superior manner with entirely new furniture, and purposes being ready for the reception of Visitors on the 10th of June next. The situation the Hotel is exceedingly beautiful, embracing from the rooms, balcony, and adjoining pleasure grounds extensive view of the Ocean and the romantic scenery of the Eastern Coast. The number of apartments exceeds 120, consisting of various suites of dining, sitting, and lodging rooms, including a magnificent Drawing room, sixty feet long. The interior arrangements are very complete, and have been formed with the object of giving (as much as would be consistent with a public establishment,) the convenience and comfort of a private residence. Hot, Cold, and Shower Baths have been fitted on the most approved plan, and can be had on the shortest notice, are easy of access and will be available also to the Visitors of the adjoining neighbourhood. The Stabling is adapted for 60 horses, the lock-up houses for 40 carriages, and the minor accommodations of the court-yard are in equal ratio. With these advantages, for a moderate rate of charge, and attentive services, J.F.S. hopes to obtain the honour of a degree of patronage commensurate with the magnitude and costly nature of his arrangements.'

Sharpin fully understood the need to offer entertainment to his guests, previously provided by the assembly rooms. A ballroom was added and opened in 1847, with the first ball being held in September of that year. Commencing at 9pm, tickets were five shillings or one pound for a family of five. During the season, the ballroom was used for many private balls. Writing in 1850, a visitor to the hotel described one such occasion:

'… the room had a very nice appearance. Mr Kholer's full band occupied the orchestra gallery. It was a grand full Dress Ball

48

The Crown Hotel, the first visitor accommodation to be constructed on the newly opened Esplanade.

and about 170 were present; some very beautiful and elegant girls, and the dresses were mostly handsome and new, we kept it up until past two o'clock with great spirit, refreshments were served up during the whole evening.... . The balls are given by the gentlemen of the Crown Hotel to the visitors of the Queen's Hotel and the Royal Hotel.'

Sharpin's lease on the Crown ran out in 1857 when a group of local businessmen took control. It has changed hands several times since but it still continues to dominate the Esplanade. It was the spur for the development for the rest of the South Cliff and especially the Esplanade 'The elegant quarter of South Cliff – a semi aristocratic preserve'.

Several other large hotels followed on from the Crown. The Royal on St Nicholas Street was expanded to include what had previously been Donnner's famous assembly rooms. Mrs Reed, its owner, had also taken over the running of the railway station refreshment rooms. The Queens Hotel, opened in 1848, overlooking the North Bay, offered over one hundred guest bedrooms. By 1860, Scarborough had many fine hotels offering accommodation at up to ten shillings per night.

The hotel which is synonymous with the town, however is the Grand. The prestigious site was originally bought by the Scarborough Cliff Hotel Company. They employed architect Cuthbert Brodrick, who had previously designed the Town Hall and Corn Exchange in Leeds. Sadly, the company's funds ran out on the difficult build and the project was finally completed by businessman Archibald Neil.

The Grand Hotel, designed around the calendar, was opened in 1867. (The US Library of Congress)

The design of the hotel was based on the theme of time, with four towers. representing the seasons, twelve floors, the months of the year, fifty-two chimneys for the weeks of the year and three hundred and sixty five bedrooms the days of the year. It was built in a V shape in honour of Queen Victoria. The interior design and furnishings were of the very highest standard, creating one of the most luxurious hotels in the world at the time. There were over thirty lounges and public rooms.

It opened in July 1867 under the management of Augustus Fricour, previously of the Hotel Mirabeau in Paris, to a tremendous flourish as the *Leeds Intelligencer* reported on 27 July of that year:

'The formal opening of the Grand Hotel in Scarborough was marked by a magnificence and brilliance quite in harmony with so palatial a structure – on the Wednesday evening by a splendid banquet and last night by a grand full dress ball, when an assembly of youth, beauty and fashion were witnessed which augers well for the future of this princely undertaking. It may be said, without an exaggeration, that if not the best it is one of the most splendid in Europe.'

Describing the interior of the hotel the article continued:

The general furnishings of the house have been executed by Messrs Smee and Sons of London. The drawing room, one of the most splendid rooms ever designed – is decorated in a most chaste manner, white, gris, perle and gold being the predominant colours.'

Access to the new hotels on the South Cliff was made much easier by the Valley Bridge, opening in July 1865. It spanned the Ramsdale Valley, linking the development with the railway station and shopping streets. The bridge was built with private finance before being taken into public ownership in 1891. The initial toll of one halfpenny for pedestrians would have been sufficient to ensure that the area remained free of day visitors.

Access to the new hotels on the South Cliff was improved by the opening of the Valley Bridge (US Library of Congress)

By the turn of the century, the number and types of hotel had risen substantially, with some twenty large hotels and many smaller private hotels together with over one hundred apartments to let. Apartments were like lodging houses, but the visitor could choose the amount of space they occupied. This could range from a full house to a single bedroom. The holidaymakers would bring their own food which would then be cooked by the landlady. A small fee was payable for the use of the cruet etc.

Scarborough in contrast, was reluctant to move with the times and was determined to remain, first and foremost a resort for the wealthy. Hotelier Tom Laughton wrote of the period:

'At this time, Scarborough was a very class conscious town …
On the front the divisions were marked by the Spa, the

exclusive resort of the prosperous and respectable with a sprinkling of the aristocracy. In the centre, the Foreshore was where the cheap restaurants and fun palaces catered for the day trippers, and the final barrier of the Castle Hill between the South Bay and the North Bay which catered mainly for the boarding house trade.'

The first large hotel in Bridlington, the Alexandra, was built in 1866 on the North end of the Promenade on Sewerby Terrace, where it sat in stately remoteness in well maintained gardens. The building provided one hundred and twenty bedrooms and epitomised good design and comfort. Eighty more bedrooms and a ballroom were added later. An advertisement from 1872 read:

'TAYLORS ALEXANDRA HOTEL – BRIDLNGTON QUAY is the only hotel fronting the sea. This magnificent hotel which stands in four acres of pleasure grounds, sloping down to the

The Pavilion Hotel

beach is now replete having been thoroughly renovated; and visitors will find charges as moderate as those of the minor houses. Families boarded upon the most reasonable terms. Table d'Hote at 6.50 o'clock. Omnibuses, cabs and carriages at the hotel, attend all the trains at the railway station and may be hired for Flamborough.'

An advertisement for the Alexandra Hotel, the finest establishment in Bridlington.

Alexandra Hotel,
BRIDLINGTON.

Telegrams—"ALEXANDRA HOTEL, BRIDLINGTON."
Telephone—2254.

THE LEADING HOTEL
IN BRIDLINGTON.

Unsurpassed Situation overlooking Bay, Flamborough Head and Private Grounds.

Nine Hole Miniature Golf Course.   Dancing.

FULLY LICENSED.

Hot and Cold Running Water in all Bedrooms.
Open all the year round.   Heated throughout.
LIFT

Meanwhile, as its neighbour Scarborough was clinging on to its appeal to the gentry and nobility, Bridlington attracted the middle class of the day and it was at this market that the hotel was aimed. By the end of the decade there were well over two hundred hotels and lodging houses in the town.

It is perhaps appropriate at this point to mention the small resort of Saltburn by the Sea. Until 1860, Saltburn was nothing more than a hamlet set in a beautiful seascape. It was the coming of the railway to the town in 1861 that spurred Quaker businessman Henry Pease into action, with his dreams of turning the village into a new and fashionable watering place. He was also involved with the Stockton and Darlington railway and obviously saw increased profits from the venture.

One of Pease's first developments was the Zetland Hotel. The building was designed by Darlington architect William Peachy and the foundation stone for the hotel was laid by the Earl of Zetland on 2 October 1861. The first part of the hotel to be built was the stable block at the rear, a substantial building in its own right. The hotel itself was opened on the 27 July 1863. It was one of the first purpose built railway hotels in the world. The height of luxury was embodied in the fact that the hotel had its own railway platform. After Saltburn station the train continued a few yards to the rear of the hotel where guests could arrive and depart. George Tweddell's *Visitors Handbook* of 1863 described the hotel: '

'The front and sides have spacious terraces, with perforated balustrades of terra-cotta, surmounted with vases of flowers: and a neat balcony runs along the whole front of the middle storey. A semi-circular tower rises in the centre of the front, which is used as a telescope room, and is provided with another balcony; and both from the top of this tower and the balcony the view is gorgeous. The hotel contains about 90 rooms, comprising about 50 bedrooms, a large dining and coffee room, a ladies' coffee and drawing room, reading room, smoking room, billiard room etc.'

Additional land was purchased from the Earl of Zetland. A surveyor, George Dickinson was employed to produce a plan allowing as many houses as possible to have sea views. The Jewel Streets – Coral, Garnet, Ruby, Emerald, Pearl, Diamond and Amber – were built along the seafront. Although Pease's plans for Saltburn were never fully realised, the project being badly affected by an economic depression in 1875, a cliff lift, a pier, the Jewel Streets and of course the hotel, testify to the fact that Pease's dream was far from a total failure.

Two other small resorts at the foot of the Yorkshire coast became established at the same time. Hornsea had been quite a flourishing town before the coming of the railway. The improved transport links did, however, add impetus to its growth. Withernsea, on the other hand was a product of the locomotive era. Its population in 1851 had been just 109 inhabitants. By the summer of that year over 63,000 people were visiting the resort using the Hull and Holderness Railway, although the vast majority of these visitors were only there for the day. It provided an escape for workers and their families, away from the noise, grime and toil of life in Hull.

The first hotel to be built in Hornsea was the Marine. By the time of Bulmer's 1892 *Directory*, five hotels and fifty-six lodging houses and apartments were listed. The plans for the development of Withernsea were even grander, with architect Cuthbert Brodrick, later to design the Grand at Scarborough, employed to build a scheme as elegant as Scarborough or Filey. The first hotel to open was the Queens in 1855. It was a grand three-storey building set next to the railway station. Its initial success was not to last long, however and by 1902 it had become a convalescent home. The dreams of wide tree lined streets and elegant crescents, attracting the middle class to the town were never fulfilled. It has, nevertheless, always been a magnet for the people of Hull and surrounding areas, if only visiting for the day.

The town of Redcar in the north-eastern corner of Yorkshire's coastal belt, also opened its own hotel in the conjoined village of Coatham. The Victoria, was to be:

'of the best possible character; and will be adapted for the temporary or permanent residents of families, as well as for the convenience of commercial gentleman and visitors generally.

'The Hotel will contain general Coffee and Dining Rooms; Private Dining Rooms; Ladies' Drawing Room; Sitting Rooms; Bed and Dressing Rooms; Hot, Cold, and Shower Baths; Billiard and Smoking Rooms; Club Rooms; and every Hotel requirement.

'It is proposed that a portion of the Hotel shall be set apart in flats containing entire suites of rooms for the accommodation of families at stated rents per week.'

Although built, sadly the hotel never flourished as hoped. A combination of a lack of further development and depression in the iron working industry saw to that.

Visitors to the coast needed to be accommodated. The resort towns had all tried to meet these requirements, albeit with varying amounts of success. Perhaps more than anything though, the story of these houses, hotels and lodgings gives a fascinating insight into a world that is now long gone. You stand outside the Crown Hotel and you can almost hear the orchestra playing and see the elegantly attired company dancing the night away.

The Journey There (and Back!)
1733–1883

The sound of a stage coach thundering to a halt outside a hostelry would have been familiar a diversion for visitors to the coast in the eighteenth and nineteenth centuries.

By 1733, a public coach had made the journey from London to the New Globe Inn at Scarborough whilst the 24 June 1766, saw an announcement made in the *York Courant* that a:

'York and Scarborough Stagecoach on steel springs will begin on Tuesday 5 July and set out from Mr John Barber's Inn in Coney Street York every Tuesday and Mr George Blanchard's New Globe Inn in Scarborough every Wednesday and from The White Horse in Coppergate, York every Friday and Mr Stephenson's New Inn, Scarborough every Saturday where passengers will be taken.'

This was very possibly the first regular coach service between the two. Confirmation that a regular service existed is provided by *Schofield's Guide to Scarborough* of 1785 which states that Diligences ran to York every day in the week during the season, fare eleven shillings. Light coaches left at seven in the morning, reaching the Golden Lion in Thursday Market about three in the afternoon, the fare being ten shillings and sixpence. They then continued to Leeds (the Rose and Crown) arriving at seven o'clock. Diligences also ran to Hull, three times per week. A Diligence was a large four wheeled closed carriage, originally of French design, but also used widely in England in the eighteenth and nineteenth centuries. By the time of the second edition of *Schofield's Guide*, there were four services to London per week.

A stagecoach on its way from London. (James Pollard 1792–1867)

Gradually, improvements in coach design and road construction saw journey times reduced significantly. By 1800, a visitor could have journeyed between London and York in under thirty hours.

Travel by coach, however, was prohibitively expensive and the preserve of the wealthy. It was also extremely uncomfortable. The most privileged of visitors were those who could afford a post-chaise. These were designed to carry a maximum of three people all facing the direction of travel but were even more costly.

When *Baines' Yorkshire Directory* was published in 1823, coaches ran regularly from several inns and to a wider range of destinations, where connections could easily be made to other parts of the country:

From Richard Hopper's Bell Inn - Bland's Cliff
ROYAL MAIL, to York, on Mon. Wed. Fri. and Sat. at ¼ past 1 aft.
OLD TRUE BLUE, every mg. at 7, to Malton, York, Tadcaster, and Leeds, (during the season)
DILIGENCE, every Sun. and Wed. mg at 8 o'clock to Whitby.
WELLINGTON, every mng. at 7 o'clock (Sundays excepted) to Humanby, Burlington, Driffield, Beverley and Hull.

From John Houson's Bull Inn - Without the Bar
OLD TRUE BLUE, every mng at 7 o'clock to Malton, York, Tadcaster and Leeds, (during the season).

From David Nicholson's New Inn - Newboro' Street
BRITISH QUEEN, to Burlington and Hull, every Mon. Wed. and Fri. and every weekday during the season, (Sundays excepted.)

From Stephen Wright's Plough Inn - Tanner Street
PRINCE BLUCHER, every mng. (Sundays excepted) to Malton, York, Tadcaster, Leeds and Sheffield, (during the season).

Of all the inns, the Bell was held in high esteem, partly because it was the terminus for the Mail Coach. The letters on the coach were deposited at the Post office and the passengers at the inn. The coach carried a maximum of seven passengers, four inside and three on the roof. It was drawn by a team of four horses. At a time when travel by road could still be unsafe, passengers would have been reassured by the fact that the guard was armed with a blunderbuss and pistols. The handsome coach, in its black and scarlet Royal Mail livery, must have made an impressive sight as it rumbled into the town.

As far removed from the Mail Coach as you could imagine was the Stage Waggon. Rambling along between towns at a slow walking pace, it carried goods over which was spread an awning. It was slow and

The London to York Mail Coach. The mail coaches were the held in special regard especially for their added security. (British Postal Museum and Archives)

uncomfortable but it was cheap and was often used by the poor. A wealthy visitor to the resort would not have been seen anywhere near it! Of course, some visitors would have come in their own coaches or even on horseback. The variety of inns offered stabling and livery facilities for such eventualities.

Bridlington shared two of the coach routes with Scarborough; the British Queen and the Wellington. In 1828, the fares from Hull were ten shillings inside and six shillings and sixpence outside. An additional service, the Magna Charta, was introduced travelling via Driffield which was advertised has being the safer route. In Whitby, three coaches ran from William Yeoman's Angel Inn. The Royal Mail to York, the Union to Sunderland and the Dilligence to Scarborough. Two coaches operated from Filey, both running on alternate days of the week.

The alternative to road transport was to arrive by packet boat. Initially powered by sail, the arrival of the steam engine shortened journey times. It was cheaper and probably no more stomach-churning an experience than travel by coach! The boats ran a regular service calling at east coast ports carrying both goods and passengers. In 1811, a fortnightly service was operating between London and Scarborough at a cost of one pound and six shillings. By 1823, the steam powered boats the *City of Edinburgh,* the *James Watt* and the *Tourist* were calling at the port, journeying to London on Thursday morning and to Edinburgh in the afternoon. The *Tourist* also called in at Whitby. The *Scarborough Album of History and Poetry*, published in 1823, reported that a packet 'now plies between Hull and Scarborough'. The journey was completed in ten hours with a fore-cabin costing eight shillings and the best cabins twelve.

It was, of course, the coming of the railways that was to bring about the most significant increase in visitors arriving at Yorkshire's coastal towns. The railway brought the destinations within reach of the middle classes and later opened up the coast to all. It required the resorts to expand on a previously unseen scale. Following the opening of the county's first line from Leeds to Selby in 1834, the demand for access to railway network swiftly grew. The next decade saw a massive increase in the new lines being built. As early as 1834, meetings had been held in Bridlington about the possibility of building a railway from the Quay to the West Riding. Interestingly, the resultant committee report concentrated on the transportation of fish, sheep, wool and cattle. The movement of passengers was not considered important at all!

There were, though, earlier plans than these, centred around a line from Whitby to Pickering. The railway was to be horse-drawn. Building commenced in 1833 and was completed three years later. Unfortunately, steam was the power of choice on the newly opened railways elsewhere in the area. The horse drawn version was outdated from the start and any passenger traffic was insignificant. The line was eventually absorbed into the York and North Midland Railway, whereupon it was rebuilt as a conventional double track steam-worked system. The first locomotive entered Whitby station in 1847.

The year 1839 found George Hudson of the York and North Midlands Railway and his engineer George Stephenson visiting Scarborough. They put forward the idea of a railway line from York which would benefit both the port and the resort. The proposal met with fierce opposition in some quarters, not least from George Knowles, a retired engineer of Wood End. His main concern was that the railway would encourage a deluge of vagrants and those 'with no money to spend'. He believed that many wealthy and respectable visitors would be deterred from coming, concluding that 'the novelty of not having a railroad would be its greatest recommendation'.

Scarborough was the first of the resorts to act. Some months after the publication of Knowles' pamphlet, the shareholders of the York and North Midlands Railway agreed for up to five hundred pounds to be spent on a survey for the proposed line. A branch line running up to Pickering was also to be built. Despite delays due to finding an acceptable route out of York, construction began in July 1844 and work was finished within one year as Hudson himself had promised. The new line opened on 7 July 1845 to much celebration and delight. *The Leeds Mercury* dated 12 July of that year reported that:

'The festivities of that day were commenced by an excellent breakfast in the Guildhall, York, at which between 500 and 600 persons of respectability and influence from all parts of the country were present by invitation. Amongst the company were George Hudson Esq. and many other members of the railway directory...

'On leaving the Guildhall, the gentlemen walked in procession headed by Walker's Band of Music, to the railway station, wither the ladies were conveyed in private and other vehicles. At the railway station a train that consists of about thirty five first class carriages was in readiness to proceed to Scarbro' This immense chain of carriages, drawn by two engines, moved off at a quarter to eleven, attended by the band of music, Union Jacks and other banners, and amidst the excited shouts of the multitude and the discharge of cannon. Most of the carriages were new and the train presented a rich and imposing sight. 'It proceeded at a slow pace during the first five miles, and then went at a somewhat quicker pace during the remainder of the journey... .

'At every station along the line there were indications of rejoicing at the auspicious event of the day. An additional band of music joined the train at Malton and at Scarborough the day was held as a general holiday and festival. On arrival of the train at the latter place just three hours after the period when it left York, Mr Hudson was received by the Mayor and Corporation with all the display and ceremony of office, and the embankments of the line were crowded with a large concourse of spectators, amongst whom were members of some secret and benevolent societies with the insignia of their respective institutions.'

Following lunch, a procession through the town was held, including passing through a temporary triumphal arch that had been erected for the occasion. The train returned to York in the late afternoon and a dinner was held, again at the Guildhall.

Initially, the line operated three services per day in each direction. Additionally, two services operated from Pickering. One service ran on Sundays. An advertisement for the line stated that trains called at all the stations on the line and more importantly for the resort of Scarborough (and indeed Whitby and the other coastal towns) which then connected with 'trains to and from London, Birmingham, Derby, Hull, Manchester, Leeds, and the West Riding of Yorkshire, Darlington, Newcastle and the North'. A branch line from nearby Seamer down the coast to Filey followed in 1846.

The truth was that Knowles was wrong in his assumption that the railway would bring, in his opinion, the wrong type of visitor to the town. The cost of travel by train was still prohibitively expensive. With fares in 1848, costing between five shillings to travel third class in an uncovered carriage and ten shillings (first class) for a single from York, rail travel was beyond the means of the working classes for quite some time.

Scarborough railway station (Adobe Images)

Although Bridlington had been the first of the coastal resorts to discuss the possibility of a railway line to the town, nothing happened until 1845. A Royal Assent was given for the construction of a branch line from the Hull and Selby Railway. At the same time, the Hull and Selby line was leased to the York and North Midland Railway who were also planning a branch from Scarborough into the town. This gave the company almost total control over the railway lines in the area.

Although the line had been intended to run to a station in the Quay area of Bridlington, objections from residents and traders in Bridlington Town saw the station being placed between the two. Like the recently opened York to Scarborough route, the construction work was undertaken in very quick time. On 6 October 1846, the new line opened, again with much pomp and celebration.

On the morning of the opening, a procession of the good and the worthy marched from the Market Place to the station, along with two music bands. Banners carrying slogans such as 'God Save the Queen' and 'Hudson and Directors – Welcome to Bridlington' were paraded. Three locomotives and sixty-six carriages arrived at the new station at just after one in the afternoon, where a lavish lunch was given. In reply to a toast, Hudson hoped:

> 'that railways would be the means of extending the commerce of that district and above all that it would be the means of conveying thousands to that place that its invigorating breezes might confer on them renewed health.'

The railway viaduct at Saltburn looks somewhat fragile by today's standards. (US Library of Congress)

THE JOURNEY THERE (AND BACK!)

The visitors returned to Hull in the afternoon where 'a splendid dinner and banquet was given in the evening at the Music Hall at which George Hudson presided'. In Bridlington, a firework display rounded off the day.

Around a year later when the Bridlington to Filey line was opened, the missing piece in the jigsaw was in place. Linking all the major resorts with the outside world, they could now be reached from most parts of the country within a day. The railways brought increasing numbers of wealthy and middle classes visitors. Yes, they also brought families on day excursions, but one or two days per year was the maximum that a typical worker could hope for. Any more than that was for later.

In the second half of the nineteenth century, railways were opened connecting Withernsea and then Hornsea to Hull in 1854 and 1864 respectively. In the north of the county, the Stockton and Darlington Railway ran a line from Redcar to Saltburn in 1861 and this was followed in 1883 by the Whitby, Redcar and Middlesbrough Union's service running from Loftus on the coast to the Esk at Whitby. The smaller coastal towns were also now within easy reach of the travelling public and that was to be a major change!

Excursions
1840–1914

In 1846, much of the country's population had not strayed very far from the village, town or city in which they were born. Certainly, a high percentage had never seen the sea. This is confirmed in a fascinating and somewhat condescending report in the *Leeds Mercury* from that year. It states:

> 'It is interesting to walk among the knots of persons... mostly of the working classes... thus brought from inland, and to hear their observations on the various objects which meet their eye for the first time. Some of them are exceedingly naïve.'

An advertisement, in much the same vein, for rail excursions to Scarborough in the *Huddersfield Chronicle,* four years later, is clearly aimed at expanding the horizons of the older population. With the reduced fares, this inward-looking view of the world was gradually to change. More and more people travelled to the coast and elsewhere from their hometowns.

The railways began offering occasional specially reduced fares as soon as the lines opened. An early advertisement from the *Leeds Mercury* dated 7 September 1844 offered a cheap pleasure trip to Hull, followed by a sea voyage on the:

> 'large powerful London Steam Ships *Waterwatch* and *Gazelle* to Bridlington Bay ... These two steam ships, being of great size and power, afford an opportunity to the public of enjoying the refreshing breezes of the German Ocean, and the delightful scenery of the North East Coast.'

EXCURSIONS

Many railway day excursions were scheduled for Saturdays and Mondays. The former was usually the day on which workers were paid, whilst the latter took account of the old tradition of Saint Monday. This was a custom of absenteeism on Mondays, common across craft workers and others, since the seventeenth century. With the adoption of half day working on Saturdays in mid-nineteenth century allowing longer weekends, the practice of absenteeism went into decline.

The affluent seasonal visitors of Scarborough and Filey, however, were in no hurry to share their coastal idylls with the working classes. They believed that with the trippers would come drunkenness, noise and indeed a disregard for the Sabbath Day. The fact that Sunday was the only non-working day for many was beside the point. The workers were supported by the National Sunday League who campaigned for the day to be special, when the employees could escape from their daily grind. Whereas many resorts were trying to woo the textile workers, miners and steel workers of Yorkshire and Lancashire, Scarborough remained steadfast in its aim of attracting the prosperous visitor.

This, did not mean that the 'trippers' were absent from the resort altogether. By 1860, groups of working class visitors were spending a day or even a weekend at Scarborough and other east coast resorts. Bridlington eventually became so attractive to the steel and colliery workers of the southern West Riding, that it was known as 'Sheffield by the sea'.

The regional newspapers were filled with special offers from the various railway companies and other organisations such as the one below from the Leeds Sunday School Union offering a 'Cheap Trip' to Scarborough for the teachers, scholars, and friends of the schools in the union. Fares ranged from five shillings and sixpence First Class to two shillings and threepence for scholars aged between twelve to sixteen. Even these prices would have been beyond the reach of many. A full day had been arranged as the notice confirmed:

'A Steamer has been engaged for trips out to the sea, and the use of bathing machines for the scholars with tea on a spacious green, having a panoramic view of the sea under the direction of a gentleman from Leeds, by whom every endeavour will be made to ensure comfort and give satisfaction. Tickets for scholars including bathing, tea and steamer fourpence: Teachers including tea and steamer fourpence; Friends including tea and steamer sixpence.'

Special hymns were written featuring the railways as a metaphor for the journey to heaven:

> 'O, What a deal we hear and read
> About railways and railway speed,
> Of lines which are, or may be made;
> And selling shares is quite a trade.
> Jesus is the first engineer,
> He does the gospel engine steer;
> "My son," says God, "give thee my heart;
> Make haste or else the train will start."'

A year later, the Hull to Bridlington line was offering 'Cheap Excursions During Whitsuntide – Passengers conveyed for one fare only'. Interestingly, the travel offer applied to the use of scheduled regular trains and not specials. Apart from middle class families, the excursions proved to be popular with single men employed as clerks and in other similar jobs.

The cheap excursions were not limited to visits for the day. An advertisement on 17 July 1847 offered a 'Cheap Trip to Filey Bay' and that the committee had made 'ample arrangements for the accommodation of the company at Filey'.

Excursions by train were also popular with visitors staying in the resorts, as Edward Baker wrote in 1850:

'About 50 of us got up early to breakfast at 8 o'clock, to go by the half past 9 o'clock Train to Whitby, 47 miles, on account of the number from the Crown Hotel, the Company gave us an

Children's Corner at Scarborough, a popular spot for visitors. (US Library of Congress)

especial train, which did not stop at any one of the stations, but went through direct to Whitby.'

After looking around the town, taking lunch at a 'Confectioner's near the pier' and peeking inside Hudson's Royal Hotel, the return journey was not quite as successful:

'We returned to the station, and left a little before 4 o'clock for Scarborough. We tried the third class carriages, but after a few miles ride, were obliged to take to the 1st class carriages again, owing to the shower of small cinders driven away from the engine completely covering us.'

The excursion generally was a success, however and the view from the train was 'most grand and beautiful'.

Ultimately, it was the introduction of bank holidays that was to change the resorts and become the catalyst for the huge crowds that they eventually drew to the coast. The Bank Holiday Act 1871 was introduced by Liberal MP and Banker Sir John Lubbock. His aim was to reduce the pressure on workers with four extra days off during the year. The days chosen were Easter Monday, Whit Monday, the first Monday in August and Boxing Day. Good Friday and Christmas Day were already established holidays. The bill was passed and whilst it initially only applied to those working in banking, it quickly spread to include all workers. There were attempts to have the August holiday renamed St Lubbock's Day but it never happened.

The *Redcar and Saltburn by the Sea Gazette* records the Whit Monday of 1871 when:

'large numbers of holiday people availed themselves of the numerous cheap trips to Redcar and Saltburn; both places were crowded with pleasure seekers who evidently enjoyed themselves to the utmost in bathing, boating, and donkey riding. The day was one of unusual loveliness, the deep blue tint of the sea continuing for the whole day, and in the evening the setting sun dyed the scene with a brilliance approaching that of the sunny clime of Italy. A more beautiful day at the seaside is rarely witnessed in the very height of the summer'

The *Bridlington Free Press* commenting on the 1882 summer season had no doubts that it was the increase in the number of excursionists that was behind the resort's success:

'this has been due to the liberal provision of excursion trains and the growing desire of people to see as much of the world as the opportunities offered will permit.'

By 1896, the number of visitors arriving by train to the east coast resorts had risen substantially, with 850,277 tickets collected at Scarborough, 385,813 at Redcar, 314,484 at Bridlington, Hornsea 117,594, Withernsea 95,348 and at Filey 82,957. Many of these would

A popular place to 'stroll along the prom, prom, prom!' – The Esplanade at Redcar.

have been visiting for the day. Redcar itself could attract over 20,000 from the industrial heartland of Teeside. The streams of visitors were still not popular in all quarters. An 1891 brochure complained that:

'We have occasionally heard that Scarborough is vulgar, in consequence of the number of day excursions that run into it. There could be no more delightful spectacle than to witness the exuberant spirits, the ludicrous efforts at enjoyment, and the utter disregard of the proprieties and conventionalities of society. But they do not frequent the Spa Grounds or interfere with the pleasures of genteel society.'

Works outings were also becoming popular to both Bridlington and Scarborough – no doubt to the dismay of some. They were sometimes

Fishermen found that taking visitors around the bay was often more profitable than taking home the catch.

a gift from benevolent employers but on occasions were paid for by the employees themselves, who would have saved on a weekly basis. It was still a time when many firms were family-owned and often had closer links with their workforce. This gesture of goodwill was also no doubt paid back in improved productivity and favourable publicity. Works outings frequently left for their destination very early in the morning. They were organised on an industrial scale themselves, requiring the hiring of several trains and scores of carriages.

One of the largest influx of trippers was the 1914 works outing to Scarborough from the Bass, Ratcliffe and Gretton Brewery. The company had been bringing its workers to Scarborough and other resorts for several years. Fifteen trains pulling 225 carriages were required, with the first trip leaving Burton-on-Tent at 3.40am in the morning and at ten minute intervals thereafter. The last train to leave entered Scarborough's recently opened Londesborough Excursion

Station, especially built in 1908 to handle the demands of excursion trains, at 10am.

A special booklet was issued to each employee giving details of Scarborough's many attractions. They were issued with money to spend and a ticket for dinner at the Scarborough Aquarium, which included roast beef plus veal and ham pies. Free entry to several of the aquarium's attractions was also included.

The next day, an article appeared in the *Scarborough Evening News* entitled *Bass Folk Should be Given the Button for Behaviour.* It continued:

'The orderly conduct of thousands of excursionists at Scarborough yesterday was frequently commented on ... The great outing was a triumph of organisation, the arrangements reflecting the result of years of experience in perfecting the big movement of industrial troops for pleasure purposes.'

Sadly, the next movement of troops was to be far less enjoyable and that was to change not just the resorts but would shake Britain in general to its very foundations.

Did You Know? –
On the Beach

You may have thought that in the nineteenth century, the beach was all about bathing. Nothing could have been further from the truth. As the century progressed, visitors placed growing importance on time spent by the sea. Many of the pursuits we now take for granted stem from that late Victorian era. It was all new and exciting. Just being there and feeling the spray from the sea was something to be treasured. The alternative for many was the smog of the factory chimneys, the noise of the looms and the coal dust of the mines.

Whilst Victorian visitors favoured Scarborough and Filey, being often genteel and appreciative of the rarefied atmosphere of the spa and the museum, it does not show the whole picture. Even as early as 1803, Willian Hutton described a scene that would be familiar to a modern-day visitor. It was a treat for him to see the children at play and 'to observe the little animals in the greatest degree of health and spirits fabricating their pies and castles in the sand'. Towards the end of the era, the beach was, as Kathryn Ferry writes, 'colourful, noisy, busy and brash'. The thousands of trippers pouring from the excursion trains had to be entertained and fed, so the beach and foreshores were a perfect place to do just that. It was home to bathing machines, ice-cream (often called hokey pokey) sellers, photographic tents, tea and coffee stalls, all manner of food vendors, Punch and Judy shows and donkeys. Hawkers paraded their wares up and down the sands whilst black faced minstrels and later the pierrots performed on especially erected stages.

The *Scarborough Gazette* in 1863 reported girls with apple baskets, a Mr Bland crying 'fish, fresh cockles', competing with Mrs Hicks and her 'any fish today', whilst an Italian ice cream man was to be

Beaches were full of stalls, traders, hawkers and entertainers. (US Library of Congress)

heard bellowing, 'Hokey pokey a penny a lump, that's the stuff that makes you jump'.

Ice cream, which had once been an expensive treat was transformed into a working-class favourite with the invention of industrial refrigeration. Many of the makers were of Italian descent such as Alonzi in Scarborough and the Trillo family in Whitby. In the early days, ice cream was sold in a glass container which was then washed before the next customer used it. Concerns about hygiene led to the development of the ice cream cone and nothing better has been found since.

Beach photographers were seen from the 1850s but were popular from the end of the century. At a time when people did not own a camera of their own, it was possible to return home with a permanent record. At first, the photographers were tied by the sizable plate cameras that they used to portable booths or tents that they set up on the sands or very nearby. They also often contained a portable darkroom. As photographic equipment became more manageable, the photographers roamed the beaches. Prints were quickly made and sold to the customer.

From the 1920s, the business of beach photography became far more professional. In 1923, the *British Journal of Photography* printed:

> 'Your picture while you wait will soon be a lost phrase at the seaside, where the antiquated "studios on wheels" are quickly vanishing from sight. Most up-to-date resorts are this year leasing exclusive beach photography rights to the modern "reflex" man, who has no use for mobile darkrooms and unnatural backgrounds. The 'reflex' man has other methods. He doesn't pose his customers, but wades into the water, snapshotting the bathers in perfectly natural attitudes. Then he exhibits prints at his stall on the beach and waits for the orders to roll in.'

It also became the accepted practice that a photographer would turn up at small hotels or boarding houses and take photographs at meal times.

Punch and Judy shows were for many years a popular attraction on many beaches up and down the country. It is believed that the first performance in this country took place in Covent Garden, London in 1662 and was witnessed by Samuel Pepys. He wrote in his diary:

> 'Thence to see an Italian puppet play which is within the rayles there, which is very pretty, the best I ever saw, and great resort of gallants.'

Based on the Italian *Commedia dell'arte* figure of Pulcinella, the character evolved into Mr Punch. His wife, was initially named Joan before changing to the catchy Judy. Originally marionettes, the puppets

78

became glove versions as the shows became more mobile and operated by one man from inside a booth or tent. Originally aimed at an adult audience, it was in Victorian era that the show changed to one for children.

The trend for Victorian families to visit the coast was a perfect opportunity for the puppeteers – often called Professors – and it wasn't long before they could be found on beaches up and down the country. By Edwardian times, the tents had become the red and white striped booths that were so familiar.

Many of the characters from that time such as the crocodile and the baby are still in the shows that remain today. With the wane of the English seaside holiday in the 1970s, the Punch and Judy show also declined and are now far from common.

Punch and Judy, a beach favourite up until the 1980s. (Adobe Images)

Minstrel shows were popular from the mid nineteenth century. The all-male shows featured performers whose faces were blackened with the aid of burned cork. The talented concert party performed on the beach to an enthusiastic audience. An important part of the troupe was the 'Uncle' figure who organised games and competitions for the children. The minstrels sang songs, played instruments, including banjos and fiddles, told jokes and generally entertained the assembled crowds.

Until just before the turn of the century, the minstrels had a virtual monopoly on beach entertainment. This was broken when Clifford Essex introduced the pierrots to England in 1891. The total antithesis of the minstrels, faces whitened with zinc oxide, and spotlessly dressed in pure white ruffled costumes with black pom poms, they had a romance and elegance that was missing from the minstrels. First performing in the Isle of Wight, they quickly gained popularity and troupes developed throughout the country.

The early pierrots earned their living busking, with a technique they called 'bottling'. The 'bottler' was a real asset to the troupe, who, through his charm and guile, could always extract a further coin from a member of the audience into his box or bottle. The profits were then shared between the troupe. For a good many years, the pierrots performed on an area of the beach, known as their 'pitch'. Eventually boards were added and later open air stages were erected. The entertainers performed up to three shows a day, usually one in the morning and two in the afternoon. As electric lighting became more widespread, evening performances gained in popularity. The pierrots were not welcome by everyone and in Whitby were unceremoniously banished from the upmarket West Cliff back to the beach.

The years progressed, and as the pierrots became more and more professional with their shows becoming more sophisticated, some moved from the beach and into theatres, floral halls and the piers. They evolved into 'concert parties' including women performers for the first time. Many famous entertainers of the 1920s and 30s cut their teeth as members of a pierrot troupe; for instance, Arthur Askey, Max Miller, and Stanley Holloway.

Catlin's Pierrots at Scarborough.

Pierrots and concert parties were always popular on the Yorkshire coast and some rose to great fame and success. Troupes performed at every resort from Redcar down to Withernsea. Perhaps the name most associated with the pierrot tradition was Will Catlin (real name William Fox).

Catlin started his career in Scarborough in 1894 where his troupe 'Catlin's Favourite Pierrots' performed on the sands. They were later to become famous throughout the country as 'Catlin's Royal Pierrots'. His performers were all male, who he portrayed as available bachelors, adding to the attraction for the many female members of the audience. He was extremely unusual in that he provided year-round employment for his cast by touring inland towns and cities during the winter months. Eventually, he ran a string of Pierrot troupes, under different managers, and owned or leased several theatres including Scarborough's Arcadia.

One of the most famous of the concert parties were the 'Fol-de-Rols'. In 1907, George Royal had brought a troupe, the 'Troubadours' from Blackpool to Whitby, changing their name to the 'Imps' in the process. No doubt after seeing the success of Catlin's troupe, he moved them once again, this time to Scarborough where they became the 'Fol-de-Rols'. They became national favourites and numerous shows under the same name were produced throughout the country, continuing to perform until well after the Second World War.

The beaches were a hive of activity and in some ways even more so than today. They provided the visitors, especially those visiting for the day, with a constant stream of refreshment, amusement and entertainment.

Recreation and Amusement
1730–1900

Writing in 1730, a traveller to Scarborough had observed that the taking of the waters was not the first thing on many visitors' minds and that 'amusements and the pleasure of seeing company induces many to come who are not really in want of water'.

Several years earlier, there had been precious little else to do in the town. The first two assembly rooms to open were on Low Westgate (now Princess Street) about which little is known and another on Sandside. Run by George Chapman, it had an elegant façade with open arches facing the sea. The most famous of the assembly rooms was the Long Room built on St Nicolas Gate, in the fashionable upper

Looking out to sea has always been a popular pastime on a day to the coast – but perhaps not dressed like this.

town. This became so well known that the street name was eventually changed to Long Room Street.

In one of his letters back home to London, the author of letters to his friend in 1733, writes:

'The High Street is called Newborough, out of which runs another up to the Long Room, which stands towards the end of the town, on the top of a cliff, from whence, by a gradual descent, you go down to the Spaw: This is a noble spacious building, fifty two feet long, thirty wide, and fifteen high; the situation being so lofty, commands a prospect over the sea, and you may sit in the windows and see the ships sailing at several leagues distance. Here are balls every evening, when the room is illuminated like a Court Assembly… Gentlemen only, pay for dancing one shilling each. On one side of the room is a music gallery, and at the lower end are kept a Pharo Bank [a French card game], a Hazard Table [a gambling game played with two dice], and Fair Chance, and in the side rooms, Tables for the such of the company, as are inclined to play at cards: below stairs you have billiard tables.'

Food wasn't forgotten:

'It is kept by Mr. Vipont, Master of the Long Room at Hampstead. There is no Ordinary here, but Gentlemen may have any things dressed in the most elegant manner, being provided with cooks from London. Everything is conducted in the most politest manner by Vipont, who is a perfect Master of his business. Gentlemen and Ladies subscribe here likewise five shillings.'

A further Long Room was opened in 1735, slightly to the north of Vipont's establishment under the management of a Mr Lewin. An entry in the diary of George Harris for 6 August 1748, gives an indication of the entertainment that was on offer:

Elegant balls were held every evening in the Assembly Rooms.

'Concert for Sigra Galli's Benefit at Lewin's. Sir Lionel Pilkington played the harpsichord – Featherstone the Violoncello.'

The singer sang two oratorio songs but Scarborough's musical preferences were not to Mr Harris' satisfaction:

'the taste for music here is quite vulgar, nothing but light unintelligible Italian airs captivate their trifling ears.'

By 1783, the Long Room which had given its name to the street, was being run by Edward Donner, whilst Lewin's was now owned by William Newstead. Rather than being run in competition, the two operated together with just one set of subscriptions and one Master of Ceremonies, Robinson Farside. Balls and other events were carefully planned to avoid clashing with each other. By 1796, Newstead had died and his rooms had closed; Donner's was the only assembly room still operating. It was still able to cater for the 'persons of the finest fashion and taste; for whole entertainment and grand dinners'. The popularity of the assembly room was, however, declining, as other forms of entertainment found favour.

Afternoons in Scarborough were often spent watching one of the plays performed initially by Thomas Keregan's Company. In 1733, he was allowed to erect a 'large booth for his comedians' together with 'scenes and decorations'. It was situated by the Crown and Sceptre Inn. Keregan was a manager of some repute and in 1734, he had been encouraged by the corporation to open a theatre close to the Minster in York. The company moved to a site on which York's current Theatre Royal now sits; it was the city's first permanent theatre.

Following the ending of the play, it was the usual custom 'to go to the Long Room again, where they dance or play till about nine and then sup in company again'. Not everyone found the company to their liking! Sarah, Duchess of Marlborough maintained her usual tone when writing to her granddaughter. 'There is no company here that one would not choose rather to be deaf and dumb than to be with them', calling them 'as dismal as a funeral'.

In 1768, Kerrigan's construction was replaced by James Caldwell's new theatre on the same site. In *Schofield's Scarborough Guide* the building is described as 'neat and compact, adequately proportioned for entertaining the company, town and neighbourhood'. Caldwell himself, comes in for special praise for his own poetical essays and songs. Plays were performed on alternate nights throughout the season, with Shakespeare always being exceedingly popular, as were the new plays by Sheridan.

Towards the end of the century, the theatre was run by the celebrated Stephen Kemble, during which time 'its boards have been graced by the acting of some of the most popular of the London performers'. In 1825, the price of admission was: Boxes, three shillings; Pit, two shillings; and Gallery, one shilling.

The Morning Chronicle of 5 August 1809 reported that the season had opened on Monday last, when Miss Duncan appeared in *Leticia Hardy*.

'On Tuesday, she played her favourite character Juliana; and was strongly supported each night by Mr Faulkner in "Dorricourt and the Duke Aranza". Indeed, the company is both numerous and respectable, comprising as much talent as can be found in any provincial theatre. Miss Simpson evinced great life and spirit in "Little Pickle".'

The famous actor Edmund Kean appeared in *The Merchant of Venice* for four nights in October 1829.

A coffee house at the corner of Tanner Street and Newborough was in business by 1725. Gentlemen 'subscribe Half a Crown, and have the use of Pen, Ink and Paper for the season'. It was still the only coffee house, seventy-five years later. Now run by Mrs Parks, the subscription for the summer had risen to five shillings. The fee, allowed visitors to read the London and provincial newspapers at their leisure.

The year 1733 saw a bookseller's shop situated on Long Room Street where, for a subscription of five shillings, ladies and gentlemen could have 'the use of any Books during the Season and take them home to their Lodgings'. A large selection of newspapers was also available. James Schofield later opened a new bookseller's in Newborough and a seasonal book store on St Nicolas' Cliff. By the turn of the century, the Agricultural and General Library had opened its doors on King Street. This was very much the preserve of the wealthier of the towns' visitors, with membership fees and charges being set at a level which only they could afford.

Another popular diversion amongst the privileged classes was the races. The first such event was held on the South Beach in Scarborough on 19 July 1728, the main race, the Scarborough Plate, being won by the rather inaptly named Cripple. Meetings were held intermittently over the next thirty years until, by 1762, a regular four-day meeting was in place. This would most certainly have been one of the highlights of the summer season.

Visiting in 1850 Edward Baker wrote of the races:

'By luncheon time the weather had changed, the rain had ceased, and the sun came out beautifully to enable us all to go down to the Spa Saloon (the top of which was the grandstand) to be present at the first day's races, held upon the sands at low water, which commenced at half past one o'clock. They were well attended.'

In the evening, the group from the Crown Hotel attended the Grand Full Dress Race Subscription Ball at the Town Hall.

It was not until 1868 that the races were moved from the beach to a grass track on Seamer Moor. The circular ten-furlong course operated until May 1907, although flat racing had ceased in August 1893.

In Bridlington, an Assembly Room had been erected in 1766 by the landlord of the Ship Inn. In a letter to the *York Courant* in July 1766, its owner, Peter Croyser, reminded the local nobility and gentry that:

'having lately erected an assembly room contingent thereto with a pleasant prospect of the sea and completed the same in a commodious and genteel manner for the reception of ladies and gentlemen and their better accommodation in the said place, begs leave to make it known that the said room will be opened for a moderate subscription for the ensuing bathing season on Wednesday 25th instant at five o'clock in the afternoon.'

The opening was attended by a 'large and genteel company, amongst whom… were gentlemen of fortune and distinction'. Some years later, the rooms were run by Mr Cooke, the permanent Master of Ceremonies. During the season, balls were held twice a week on Tuesday and Friday. The subscription was one guinea and five shillings.

Whilst not on the same scale as Scarborough, Bridlington gradually began to evolve into a resort offering the entertainment facilities that discerning visitors required. A theatre was opened around 1805 on the Rope Walk near Chapel Street by William Smedley from Lincolnshire.

He provided theatrical entertainment to the increasing number of visitors for over twenty years.

By 1823, *Baines' Directory* listed: two booksellers; three circulating libraries; four lapidary shops; two billiard table keepers; and Ralph Stubbs, a miniature portrait painter, all of whom would have been essential to a wealthy visitor's stay in the town.

Scarborough, meanwhile, was continuing to attract the professional and cultured classes, as was shown in the building of its first public museum. The Rotunda was opened in 1829 by the Scarborough Philosophical Society to display its growing collection of fossils and minerals. The society decided to construct its own building rather than adapt a rented property. As such, it was one of the first purpose-built museums in the country. Its circular design was suggested by William Smith, known as the 'Father of English Geology'; he believed that it was the ideal way of displaying the new collections. The location of the museum below St Nicholas' Cliff, in the fashionable part of the town, was chosen to attract the affluent visitor who could afford the

The Rotunda Museum opened in 1829. (Wellcome Trust)

one shilling entrance fee. Solomon Theakston, after lamenting that many of Scarborough's buildings were unattractive, paid tribute to the new museum calling it a 'neat and beautiful repository of the remains of a former world'.

Visiting in 1839, Augustus Granville effused over the exhibition remarking that:

> 'To those that make that place [Scarborough], their place of residence for a month or two, such a museum must prove a delightful source of amusement and intellectual gratification. Every temptation ... has been offered to the scientifically minded or even to the merely curious to visit frequently.'

By this time, the entrance fee was two and sixpence for a month or five shillings for a whole family. Was this one of the earliest examples of a family ticket?

Of the former Donner's Long Room, now Reeds Hotel, Granville was not as enchanted. The ballroom was hardly used, prompting Granville to write:

> 'Of all the auxiliaries so much required at, and generally forming the boast, of other spas, Scarborough repudiates the two principal and most cheering ones – dancing and sociability.'

The first entertainment at the Spa were orchestra and band concerts. The first permanent band to play was assembled by R.W. Kohler, a music shop owner, who supplied the musicians from 1848 to 1854. He was initially paid a sum of £160 for a thirteen week season. Four years later, this had risen to £198. A succession of musical directors followed until in 1867, they appointed German born, Meyer Lutz, a professional musician, who was also appointed musical director of the Gaiety Theatre in London combining both roles until 1878.

Initially contracted to play on six mornings and four evenings, the workload gradually increased to include afternoon performances and eventually concerts on a Sunday. Musical Directors have come and

Scarborough's Spa around 1890. (US Library of Congress)

gone with perhaps the most famous being Max Jaffa, who held the post from 1960 for some twenty-seven years. Jaffa's musicianship and his carefully blended programmes of light classical with the occasional longer piece of serious music, were extremely popular. The concerts were often broadcast on BBC radio.

Paxton's improvements to the building coincided with the dawn of the music hall and variety as forms of popular entertainment. One particular and somewhat bizarre act that was a favourite at the Spa was The Two-headed Nightingale, which:

'consisted of two heads and four arms, shoulders and legs all blending into one body. She – I hardly know whether to use the singular or the plural number – sang very well soprano and contralto harmonizing sweetly, ate and drank independently, was well educated and very intelligent. One would talk to you whilst the other read a book. She was of an apparently happy disposition, running about the place between the afternoon and evening exhibitions with evident enjoyment.'

Scarborough's Music Hall evolved into the most popular outside London and was twice visited by royalty. In 1869, the Prince of Wales visited and was joined on a later visit by his wife, Princess Alexandra.

Dramatic performances were first staged at the Spa from the 1870s when actors such as Lionel Brough and Nellie Farren could be seen. The new theatre was opened in 1880 with the play *The Old Love and the New*. It was also famous for its firework displays, with the first one taking place in 1844. Brock's displays commenced in 1871. However, it was for its music that the Spa was renowned. Today, it remains the only such venue with a permanent orchestra during the summer season.

The Victoria Rooms, opened in 1848, were Bridlington's first public rooms and were for many years the town's major setting for

The castle like appearance of the Victoria Rooms is clearly seen in this view from Bridlington Harbour's East Pier. (US Library of Congress)

concerts, plays, lectures and social events. Paid for by the sale of shares, the Tudor-style rooms were situated on the North Pier by the harbour. The attraction was managed for many years by J.M. Wilson, often called the 'Professor'. He was also the conductor of the Parade Band. Entertainment ranged from full choral works to minstrels and some of the variety acts could be just as strange as those at Scarborough's Spa. The Ethiopian Burlesque Opera Troup and Colonel Harrison's Pigmies are just two. It was also used for the new cinematograph shows. The rooms were purchased by the Local Board in 1879 and by 1893 had become part of the Town Hall. The building was destroyed by fire in 1933.

The Sea Wall and Parade was opened to the north of the harbour in 1867. Fifteen years later, a guide book finds much to admire in the new development:

'The parade furnishes a beautiful marine promenade, seven hundred feet long, and tastefully enlivened with gay parterres of flowers, ornamental shrubs and everything that can be added to its attractiveness.'

By this time, a Pavilion had been added in which a band played regularly and had become a major attraction. An entrance fee of threepence was charged, which eventually rose to fourpence, for which a visitor could walk along the promenade and listen to the band.

The coming of the railways had certainly changed the make-up of the visitors to the coast. Besides the wealthy and middle classes who came for extended stays, those coming for the weekend and even a day had to be entertained. Building populist new attractions near to the exclusive area around the Spa was not without its critics. As a result, high entrance charges and tight rules regarding behaviour were to be the order of the day in an attempt to deter undesirables.

The harbour in Scarborough was separated from Ramsdale Valley by a stretch of beach. Proposals were put forward in 1866 and 1871 for a Foreshore Road. The siting of the Grand Cafe above the west end of the south sands and the Aquarium at the sea end of the valley would draw day visitors to that area. The Aquarium Company built part of the road in 1874, with the remainder being constructed on behalf of the corporation some four years later. This half a mile of carriage drive, became a well-used promenade. The area was changed from one made up of yards, chandlers and storehouses to one given over completely to the amusement of visitors to the resort.

Like so many of Scarborough's improvements and developments, it was private money that was behind the aquarium. The Marine Aquarium Company was set up in 1874 and their plans received royal assent in July the following year. The architect chosen for its design was Eugenius Birch, the brainchild behind the Brighton Aquarium, which had opened to great acclaim in 1872. The company had tasked Birch with building something bigger and better than its southern spa equivalent. The aquarium was constructed completely underground on a two and a half acre site under the Cliff Bridge, where there had previously been a stagnant pool and almost derelict horse and carriage stables. The construction was a massive undertaking, requiring the removal of 200,000 cubic yards of earth and 40,000 cubic yards of bricks and masonry. It took nearly three years and over £120,000 to complete.

The official opening was on Whit Monday in 1877. A week earlier, a preview had been held for local residents at which the press had been present. A report in the *Yorkshire Post and Leeds Intelligencer* was very enthusiastic about the new attraction, believing that visitors' verdicts on the aquarium:

'would be favourable and that Scarborough's reputation as a seaside resort would be favourably enhanced of that there cannot be a doubt.

'The interior of the building itself, independent of what the tanks contain is something to remember. The novelty of the style of architecture adopted, its moving and singular beauty and the wonderful and ever varying picturesque effects, which meet you at every turn are strikingly impressive.'

That interior was designed in a style that was described as

RECREATION AND AMUSEMENT

'Mohamedan-Indian'. Following Queen Victoria being crowned Empress of India, eastern architecture was extremely fashionable and the aquarium was certainly that. Lavishly decorated, a series of rooms led to a magnificent dining room. The aquarium housed twenty-five tanks containing fresh and saltwater fish, seals, crocodiles and other creatures. One of the tanks, with a 75,000 gallon capacity, was advertised as the largest in the world.

One of the highlights of a visit to the aquarium was the grotto. It was:

> 'Formed of tufa, built up to a height of many feet out of which ferns, Irish yews and other bright green plants and to make the deception complete a stream of water falls from the above and tumbles down into a small pond at the base of the grotto. In the centre of the grotto, the orchestra is erected and as it will always be occupied by an excellent band the central transept is sure to be a favourite for visitors.'

Beautiful and impressive as it was, the aquarium was a financial failure. The summer of 1879 was an extremely poor one weather-wise and visitor numbers were low. Coupled with the fact that excursionists were not visiting, a combination of the high price of admission and that, 'very many of the excursionists belong to a class of people who may be supposed to have little appreciation of the charms of the aquarium', by 1881 the company was virtually bankrupt. It was eventually sold at a loss to William Morgan, who was the manager of the Winter Gardens in Blackpool. Bringing with him a philosophy gained from dealing with a wider range of visitors at the west coast resort, he is reputed to have made the possibly apocryphal comment that 'visitors would rather see a juggler than an uncooked lobster'. Morgan completely redeveloped the business and the People's Palace was born.

For an admission price of just sixpence, a visitor could spend up to ten hours enjoying a wide range of entertainment ranging from instrumental and vocal concerts in the large Concert Hall and up to five variety shows per day in the Indian Theatre. He prided himself on

An advertisement for the feast of entertainment on offer at Scarborough's People's Palace – formerly the Aquarium.

the range of the acts advertising 'the best' acrobats, gymnasts, conjurors, ventriloquists and others. Some tanks were closed and replaced with stalls and sideshows. A camera obscura and a gallery of optical illusions was added.

A seventy-five foot long swimming pool was opened for public use and for swimming exhibitions including, amongst others, Ada Webb and her Champion Troupe of Lady Swimmers. The cross-Channel swimmer, Captain Webb, had also been a visitor in 1880, amazing onlookers by the length of time he could spend in a tank without harm.

A Blackpool man had turned the aquarium into Scarborough's Blackpool Tower. He had also, unashamedly, brought entertainment to the excursionist and the Foreshore was to become their playground.

The more affluent visitors preferred to remain at the Spa, the South Cliff and on the quiet beaches of the North Bay. Not surprising then, when the area was chosen as the site for another new development. The Victorians were exhibition mad and following the success of the Norwich Marine Exhibition in 1881, Caleb Petch was instructed by John Woodall to design an exhibition hall for the town. The building had 10,000 square feet of exhibition space and could seat over 5,000. A large stage was erected in the main hall, with a smaller theatre on the first floor. The first display was the Fisheries and Marine Exhibition in May 1895. Opened by General Sir Evelyn Wood V.C. it was a success and ran for the rest of the year. This was followed by a Sports, Games and Industry exhibition.

It was Morgan who was to transform the exhibition hall into a place of entertainment. True to form, a wide variety of acts were booked to appear, including flying trapeze artistes and a Turkish harem. The corporation bought the building in 1898, before refurbishing it and reopening it as the New Empire. The building changed owners, names and uses on a regular basis, with periods as a picture theatre, roller skating rink and dance hall. Now renamed Olympia, it was damaged during the First World War. It was eventually repaired and continued to be used all year round until it was destroyed by fire in 1975.

A wooden building was erected on St Thomas' Street on the site of what became the Scarborough Opera House. Known initially as Charles Adnam's Grand Circus, the building went through several incarnations before finally becoming the New Hippodrome. The auditorium was used for circus and music hall acts until its partial demolition in 1908.

Nearly fifty years after the opening of the Victoria Rooms, Bridlington was in desperate need of new sources of amusement and entertainment. The Royal Prince's Parade, like the South Cliff at Scarborough, was considered the preserve of the well to do visitor who came for the season. An admission charge ensured that excursionists tended to stay away.

1896 saw the provision of two new grand entertainment pavilions, the People's Palace on Quay Road (a concert hall with a 1500 seat capacity and a dance hall below) followed by the New Spa and Gardens. The latter were built in 1896 by the Whittaker Brothers of Horsforth in Leeds. After paying the entrance fee, visitors had access to five acres of gardens and pathways, refreshment rooms, a theatre and a glass domed bandstand. Whilst there were no facilities for taking the spa water any more, a lake was filled with water from the chalybeate spring. The opening on 27 July of that year was reported in the *York Herald*. Whilst the large concert hall was not quite finished in time for the ceremony, it allowed visitors to appreciate its size and appearance. Both the new licenced refreshment rooms and Fields café were doing good business.

The report describes the new gardens where:

'seats have been placed around the bandstand and in various other parts of the grounds, together with rustic summerhouses. The flowerbeds had been filled up and looked exceedingly pretty.'

Shops in the colonnade sold a wide variety of fancy goods, fruit and flowers whilst on the miniature lake model boats were sailing back and forth. The most important aspect of the opening day was the music. Veteran conductor Herr Lutz – formerly of Scarborough – with his band, opened with the National Anthem and entertained the crowds for over two hours. He was followed by the band of the 17th Lancers. A grand firework display rounded off the evening with the grounds being 'illuminated with variegated lamps'.

The Spa proved to be a success and at one point, 80,000 people passed through the turnstiles in just one month. Like its namesake in Scarborough, the Bridlington version was to become the primary source of quality entertainment in the town.

In the smaller resorts, the growth in places of entertainment was much more low key. Built in 1880 by Sir George Elliot, Whitby's West Cliff Saloon offered a selection of both concerts and plays during the summer season, whilst the Promenade was home to daily band performances.

The Crescent Gardens, Filey.

In Filey, the Crescent Gardens, had, since the 1860s, been the home of band concerts, where they were initially performed in the open air until a band stand was erected in 1872. There was perhaps someone who was not a music lover, for several years later the structure was burned to the ground in an arson attack. Up until the 1960s, except for a break during the 19390-45 war, the gardens were home to a series of small orchestras and even to open air dancing.

It is again worth making a special note of Saltburn-by-the-Sea. The would-be resort was full of grand plans and after several false starts the town opened its Assembly Rooms in 1885. Designed by Alfred Waterhouse of London, the hall's initial concert was held on Friday 10 July. With seating for over 600, the building was considered one of the best of its type in the country. Eventually the building was to be extended and modernised before being renamed the Spa Pavilion.

Prior to this date, the major source of recreation in Saltburn, previously the Valley Gardens, opened in three stages in the period 1860-1871. The bulk of the pleasure grounds were designed by John Newton, whose proposals included extensive tree planting, a croquet

The Italian Gardens in Saltburn. (Adobe Images)

lawn, a bandstand with banked seating, a network of woodland paths and steps linking the existing lower and upper paths, two new entrances with pay booths at the coast, the Albert Memorial, several summerhouses, seating, and a formal Italian Garden.

At the turn of the century, Scarborough and Bridlington had begun to offer the visitors to their towns the entertainment they craved. Such facilities were a necessity if they were to tempt holidaymakers and excursionists away from Blackpool and Morecambe, which had been attracting the working classes in their droves. Whilst the smaller resorts of Whitby and Filey were some way behind them, what they did provide was perhaps in keeping with their size and the visitors they were keen to attract. Little has been said up to now about the other fledgling resorts. Whilst they possessed little in the form of theatres, halls and other palaces of entertainment, there was one thing that they all offered, albeit with varying amounts of success, and that was a seaside pleasure pier.

Yorkshire's Pleasure Piers

A visitor to the Yorkshire coast today will find only one example of that unique form of architecture, the pleasure pier. Clinging to life against all the elements that the North Sea can throw at it, Saltburn-by-the-Sea pier is the last remaining of six such piers that were dotted in resorts up and down the county's coast.

Ryde, in the Isle of Wight, was the first resort to build a landing pier back in 1814. This was followed just nine years later by Brighton's elegant chain pier, which was soon recognised not only as a landing pier, but as a place to promenade up and down – a fashionable place to see and to be seen. In short, the pleasure pier was born.

It was Henry Pease and the Saltburn Improvement Company's inspired resort that was the first of the Yorkshire coastal towns to consider building a pleasure pier. In 1861, the construction had been approved but it was not until 1867 that work commenced under the auspices of engineer John Anderson. Connected with both the Stockton and Darlington and the South Durham and Lancashire Union Railways, he sensed profits were to be made in the evolving resort and had bought large plots of land as they became available. He was responsible for the construction of the Alexandra Hotel, which at the time was considered almost on a par with the nearby Zetland.

In January 1867, Anderson was appointed both engineer and contractor of the Saltburn Pier Company, which he had formed alongside John Bell, Edmund Grove and James Taylor. The first delivery of the ironwork arrived from Cochrane and Grove of Oremseby and on 30 December of that year work commenced. According to the *Newcastle Courant,* the first pile of the new pier was driven in by Mrs Thomas Vaughan of Gunnergate near Middlesbrough.

The cast iron pier with wooden decking was 1500 feet long and some 20 feet wide, with a landing stage for the use of pleasure

Saltburn Pier was opened to much acclaim in May 1868. (US Library of Congress)

steamers and other small boats. On the land side were two grand hexagonal entrance kiosks. It was to much acclaim that the pier opened to the general public in May 1869. Steam boat trips to Scarborough and Bridlington operated regularly in the summer months, as well as travelling further up the coast to Hartlepool. Bands entertained those waiting for their sailings as well as the many visitors who were content just to saunter up and down the new attraction taking in the fresh sea air. A saloon serving refreshments was opened in 1871.

The pier proved to be an instant success, with 50,000 people visiting in the first six months. To boost attendance even further, the Pier Company erected a 120 feet high vertical cliff hoist, which could take up to twenty passengers at a time up and down the cliff. Looking at it now, it appears an extremely precarious structure. It must have worked, however, as it operated effectively for years until its demise in 1883.

For the first three years after its opening, the pier made a profit but by the end of 1873 that return was rapidly diminishing. When a severe storm hit the town in 1875 and badly damaged both the landing stage and much of the seaward end of the pier, there was no money left to pay for the repairs. A loan that the company could ill afford was taken out, allowing the restoration to be completed in 1877. The length of the pier was reduced by 250 feet and the supporting iron structures strengthened to prevent further damage. Upon its reopening, the pier was once again in profit. Even so, it was not to last and by 1879 the Saltburn Pier Company was in liquidation. The running of the pier was taken over by the Saltburn Improvement company who set about refurbishing and improving the attraction, adding a bandstand together with seating shielded by glass partitions plus refreshment rooms with new and more substantial buildings at the entrance.

The other major improvement was the replacement of the cliff hoist system with a cliff tramway, allowing an easier and far less 'perilous' journey up and down to the town. The funicular, still in operation today, rises 120 feet, runs on 207 feet of track at an incline of 71 per cent. The two cars carried between ten and twelve people and were fitted with beautiful stained glass windows. The *South Durham and Cleveland Mercury* reported that:

'The new inclined tramway, which for some time past has been in course of formation is now in working order. Several trips were made on Monday quite successfully. The enlargement of the pier is nearly complete, and the new headway with its prettily designed windscreen, cannot fail to be highly appreciated.'

In 1887, gas lighting was replaced by electricity.

The pier became a symbol of Saltburn's popularity as a seaside resort, with thousands visiting, especially from the north east of England. Listening to the band, promenading and even fishing in the sea below were popular pastimes. Operations ran smoothly until the night of 7-8 May 1924, when the vessel *Ovenbeg*, carrying a cargo of china clay from Fowey in Cornwall, repeatedly collided with a section of the pier during a storm. The result was a 210 feet wide gap. Temporary measures were put into place allowing the front section of the pier to be used. It was not until five years later that it was fully restored, with the addition of a theatre on the landside.

Bought by the Saltburn and Marske Urban District Council in 1938, it was requisitioned two years later by the army and a large section of the pier was removed to prevent its use in the event of an invasion. Lack of maintenance over this period saw the condition of the pier deteriorate rapidly and the end of the war found it in an extremely poor condition. Debates about who should foot the bill for the pier's restoration and a shortage of steel, culminated in the repair work not being undertaken until 1947. It was eventually reopened to the public in 1952 at a cost of £20,000. It was reported that 20,000 people visited it in the first month. The year following saw another chapter in the pier's chequered history, when once again a storm resulted in severe damage to its structure. Further repairs were completed five years later at a cost of £23,000.

Once re-opened, the pier always remained popular with up to 90,000 visitors a year. The 1970s saw further problems on a regular basis, mainly with the supporting piles and the rusting of the steel work in general. The continuing problems culminated on 29 October 1974 when the pierhead was destroyed in a severe storm and much of the remaining structure was badly damaged. With the pier declared unsafe, the local council applied to the Department of the Environment for permission to demolish it. There was an outcry in the town and a public enquiry was held in November 1975. Following recommendations that only the thirteen end trestles should be removed, restoration work began again in 1976 with the pier being reduced to 681 feet in length. The pier was reopened to the public on 29 June 1978, the entrance now restored, enclosing an amusement arcade and café. Further renovation was undertaken in the 1990s. The culmination of all this hard work and expense was when the pier was highly placed in the Queen's Golden Jubilee Heritage Awards and was subsequently awarded Pier of the Year in 2009. Martin Easdown of the National Piers Society wrote that:

The pier and cliff lift are still operating today. (Adobe Images)

'Saltburn Pier has had probably, the most turbulent history of any surviving pier in Britain today ... Long may she continue to provide relaxation and entertainment to people for many years to come.'

Around the same time that Saltburn was deliberating on the construction of a pier, Scarborough was thinking along the same lines. A proposal was first put forward by a group of Manchester businessmen in 1864 to erect a pier in the South Bay. Due to the usual objectors, who believed that the wrong type of visitors would be attracted and the Board of Trade, who were worried that it would be a hazard to shipping, the plan was abandoned.

The next plan to be put forward was by local banker, John Woodall. A company was formed in 1865, with the majority of the investors being local businessmen and hoteliers. Surprisingly, their plan was to build the pier on the North Bay which at this time, was still in the main undeveloped. Eugenius Birch, who was to later design Scarborough's Aquarium building, was employed to engineer the pier and on the 14 September 1866, the first pile was driven in to the ground. The construction was riddled with delays, partly due to the untimely death of the main contractor, J.E. Dowson.

By 1 May 1869, thankfully the pier was completed at a cost of over £12,000. It was 1,000 feet in length. A shelter at the pier head allowed for band concerts to be held and refreshments to be served. Alas – the pier was not successful. Visitor numbers were low, dividends paid to investors were minimal and the company was in debt to local banks. On top of this, a decision was made to ban steamers from calling at the pier head owing to the constant damage they were causing. A vital source of both income and visitors was therefore lost.

A series of near disasters in the 1880s when the pier was hit by the steamers, the *Star* and the *Hardwick* together with the yacht *Escalpa* did not help matters. Gales in 1883 had also blown the shelter into the sea. The pier was in a mess and receipts plummeted. The closure of the cliff tramway opposite the pier was the final straw for the investors and the pier was sold to Walter Hudson of London for just £1,240. He then invested £10,000 renovating the pier, including enlarging the pier head and erecting a pavilion upon it. The tollbooths were replaced by a handsome new building including a restaurant. *An illustrated Guide to Scarborough the Beautiful* was enthusiastic about the refurbished pier:

'The Promenade Pier, in the North Bay is, a very alluring resting place , affording all the pleasures of a sea trip without any of its discomforts. It possesses a spacious concert hall where variety entertainments are kept going all through the season; excellent restaurant, refreshment saloons etc., and not a few visitors to Scarborough spend the entire day on its delightful promenade.'

The pier never attracted the number of visitors it should have and even the introduction of performers of the calibre of Marie Lloyd did little to enhance its financial success.

The pier was purchased for £3,500 in 1904 by William Morgan, who by then was mayor of the town. He was not to own it for long. On 6 January 1905, a combination of a severe north westerly gale and a very high tide saw the pier destroyed apart from the pavilion, which was cast adrift several hundred feet from the shore. The pier was not insured and was never rebuilt.

The resort of Redcar was the next east coast town to build a pier. The resort had been expanding since the 1850s, with a seawall and promenade having been constructed in the following decade. Whilst discussions about the erection of a pier had been ongoing for some time, it was not until neighbouring twin-town Coatham had put forward proposals for a pier of its own, that action was taken. After negotiations to construct a joint pier, sited centrally between the towns had failed, both towns decided to build their own.

The pier was designed by J.E. & A. Dowson, who had been the original contractors on the building of the pier at Scarborough. When J.E. Dowson died in 1868, Head Wrightson & Co. of Stockton were instructed to construct it, the building being financed by the sale of shares and by contributions from the Earl of Zetland.

The first pile was ceremoniously driven into the sand in August 1872 by Admiral Chaloner of Guisborough, one of the directors. Its official opening eighteen months later was reported in the *Redcar and Saltburn-by-the-Sea Gazette*:

'Whit Monday (2 June) was a day of high rejoicing at Redcar, when thousands of people from various parts of the country assembled to witness the opening of Redcar Pier. Notwithstanding the threatening condition of the weather on the previous day, and even on the morning of Monday, before noon the atmosphere cleared, and the streets were thronged with spectators to witness the procession of Directors, Shareholders, Inhabitants and Visitors.'

The report continued to describe the pier as being 1,300 feet in length and 20 feet in width. The pier head widened out to 114 feet wide and featured a bandstand with seating for 700 behind protective shields. There was also a separate landing stage for the passengers of the pleasure boats. It was estimated that upwards of 4,000 people visited the pier on the first day and 1,350 on the following day.

Sadly, Redcar Pier like others on the Yorkshire coast was to be at the mercy of the sea and the stormy weather. On 8 October 1875, a severe gale hit the coast resulting in damage to both Redcar and Saltburn Piers:

'On Friday morning a large quantity of timber was noticed on the sands above Redcar, leading to the belief that some vessel must have been wrecked, but it was found to have belonged to Saltburn Pier, part of which was washed away. In the afternoon one of the wooden girders of Saltburn Pier, about thirty feet in length, with two large pieces of ironwork attached, was noticed among the breakers off Redcar Pier Head, and about four o'clock it struck with tremendous force against the east side of the pier, breaking off one of the cast iron columns, and afterwards getting entangled in the column opposite the one broken, against which it struck with every sea. Efforts were made to remove it by means of grappling irons and ropes. As it was feared greater damage would be done, but in vain; it was left to be tossed about with the waves till the tide had ebbed sufficient for it to be removed.'

Further damage was incurred on 28 October 1880 when the ship *Luna* was driven by a severe storm into the pier, resulting in damage estimated at over £1,000. Significant damage was also incurred further south at Hornsea and Withernsea Piers. On the last day of 1885, a steamer, the SS *Cochrane*, ran into the pier and demolished the landing stage. Without it, steamers were unable to use the pier.

Additional damage was caused in January 1897 when wreckage from an abandoned ship, the Norwegian Schooner *Amarant*, hit the

Redcar Pier. (US Library of Congress)

pier resulting in a sixty feet long tear. This was quickly repaired. Things though were set to get worse when in August of the next year, the pier head was burned down. The incident was covered in the *Leeds Mercury.*

'At present Redcar is filled with visitors from various parts of Yorkshire and Durham, the season being at its height. Both residents and visitors have had an unfortunate experience in the destruction by fire of the pier head, saloon, bandstand and office adjoining. The Hemming Concert Party have been giving entertainment daily on the pier to thousands of visitors. On Friday night, some 500 or more people were on the pier listening to the concert and at half past nine (closing time) nothing was observed with the pier. It is believed that some smoker had carelessly dropped a lighted match on the pier deck, and that it fell below and smouldered for some time before breaking into flames. The pier had been cleared when Mr Hemming Jnr. observed a fire under the pier deck. He hastened onto the pier and with other helpers tried to extinguish the fire with buckets of sea water. The Redcar Fire Brigade and the Coatham manual fire engine were soon on the spot, but unfortunately no water could be procured and the woodwork of the pier head including the bandstand and offices were rapidly burnt away.'

The bandstand was not replaced, but seating was reassembled on the new pier head, the total cost of the repairs being in the region of £1,500. In due course, the Pavilion Ballroom was built behind the entrance kiosks. This dancehall was extended in 1928 and a tearoom added. The pier existed trouble free up to the Second World War when, like many others, it was breached to prevent German access in the event of an invasion. During the war, a mine exploded near the pier resulting in significant damage. Already weakened, further storms made matters worse and by the end of the war only forty-five feet remained. Redcar Pier was sold to the Borough Council and £4,500 spent on renovating what remained of it. The future of Britain's smallest pier was far from secure, but somehow it worked and the years up to the latter end of the 1970s were some of the pier's best. By 1980, however, the pier was considered unsafe and the decision was made to demolish it by Christmas of that year.

Construction of a rival pier at nearby Coatham eventually commenced in 1873. The pier was to be 2,000 in length, over 700 feet longer than the one at Redcar. In December of 1874, with the work nearly completed, a catastrophe happened that almost ended the project before it had started. In the middle of a storm with waves of tremendous height crashing towards the shore, not one but two vessels struck the pier. The *Redcar and Saltburn-by-the-Sea Gazette* recounted the night's events.

'Nothing serious, however, occurred until nearly 4 o'clock, when the brig *Griffen*, of Southampton (William Mundy, master), cut through the Coatham Pier between the saloon and the entrance, carrying away girders and columns, and making a tear in the promenade about 100 yards in extent.'

All the crew managed to survive the terrifying ordeal by jumping from the ship onto the pier as it crashed through it. The vessel eventually drifted away from the pier and became fast in the sand. The schooner *Corrymbus* was driven into the pier nearer the promenade. The crew were all saved but the ship was lost. In all, five vessels ran ashore during the night. The cost of repairing the pier was enormous and to save on costs its length was reduced by 200 feet.

The pier did eventually open in 1875 to some acclaim. It contained two pavilions, one at the centre of the pier and another inside the entrance. Used for band concerts and other amusements, the pier was quite striking. It was not, however, financially successful and was vulnerable to the vagaries of the weather. As such operating costs were high. It was badly damaged a year after its opening, when a storm resulted in the loss of a length of pier some 200 yards long. The repairs were estimated to cost around £3,000.

The final nail in the pier's coffin, however, was in 1898, when on the 22 October the pier was once again severed, this time by the storm damaged Finnish barque *Birger*. The tragedy that unfolded was watched by a crowd of several thousand onlookers who had gathered on the promenade to view the ship breaking up. Two Lifeboats were launched, the Redcar crew in their boat *The Brothers* and the Free Gardeners in *Emma*.

The local paper movingly recounted the terrible events:

'First it seemed as though the mighty breakers would be too powerful for them, sweeping them back as though to dash them to destruction on the Coatham pier. But the hearts of such men were not to be daunted, the resistance they met with, only causing them to double their efforts, gradually reducing the distance between themselves and their intended goal. The wind, which was blowing in a slanting direction, made their task very difficult, and from the onset the attempt at rescue seemed futile. In the meantime, the vessel struck with a terrific crash, and the work of demolition began in earnest. The fore and mizzen masts came down with a crash, and the terrible seas swept the wreck from end to end. The crew of the vessel were clustered under the bulwarks in the stern, and it was purely a matter of time. The lifeboat crew fought on in their superhuman efforts to reach the wreck – when, within a short distance, the end came. The mainmast fell, the hull divided, and, in the place where less than an hour before there was a fine three-masted barque, there was now just a tangled mass of wreckage.'

All but three of the crew were killed. The survivors had clung on desperately to a piece of wreckage. Attempts were made to lift them out of the sea and onto the pier but sadly one of men, exhausted, fell back into the sea and drowned. Another was washed up on to the beach whilst the third scrambled his way on to the pier. He was rescued just in time as:

'Immediately after the man was drawn on Coatham Pier by the line, there was a cry in the crowd that a raft was coming and they had only time to get clear when a large quantity of wreckage crashed into the piles where they had been standing and made a breach of some 100 yards in length. Had they not received the warning, a most terrible calamity must have happened.'

The owners of the pier were unable to meet the cost of the substantial repair bill and the seaward section of the pier was demolished. When the Coatham Pier Company went out of business the pier was left to rot, eventually being dismantled some years later. A sad end to a town's big dreams.

The last two piers to be built were in the south of the region at

Withernsea and Hornsea. The coming of the railways had opened the towns up for development. In the case of the former, this was championed by Alderman Anthony Bannister who formed the Withernsea Pier, Promenade, Gas and General Improvement Company. The company's prospectus included a commitment to erect a pier in the town, the entrance of which would be situated half way along the promenade. This, along with the rest of the development never got off the ground. New plans were drawn for a pier to be built opposite the railway station. This was situated further to the south of the town with Thomas Cargill, who had previously designed the pier at Aldeburgh in Suffolk, as the engineer and J.O. Gardiner, as the contractor.

Despite some damage during its construction, the 1,196 feet long pier was completed by August 1877. Built entirely out of iron, except for the brick entrance and wooden decking, the pier used the new technology of screw piles, which were driven deep into the ground. Seating was provided along the full length of the pier and a saloon and hall for entertainment was situated at the pier head. The entrance to the pier consisted of two castellated towers, rumoured to be based on Conwy Castle in Wales.

Upon opening in August 1878, the pier quickly became profitable. The one penny admission charge ensured that it was accessible to all and not just a select few. Excursionists, especially from nearby Hull, flocked to the new attraction. Unfortunately, the success of the pier was to be short-lived.

On 28 October 1880, a devastating storm erupted which caused damage to many of Yorkshire's piers. Withernsea Pier suffered twice when it was hit by two separate, storm damaged vessels. The fishing smack *Jabez*, operating out of Colchester, hit the end of the pier, sinking with the loss of the four men on board. Three of the four sailors are buried in Saint Nicholas Churchyard in Withernsea, with the fourth buried at nearby Holmpton, where his body was washed up on the shore. The Withernsea memorial to those brave sailors reads:

'Sacred to the Memory
of
GEORGE KETTLE
AGED 41 YEARS
GEORGE FITCH
AGED 21 YEARS
WILLIAM CANT
AGED 18 YEARS
ALSO **JAMES JOHN LAMB**
AGED 33 YEARS
WHO IS INTERRED AT HOLMPTON
NATIVES OF COLCHESTER WHO WERE DROWNED IN THE
STORM OF OCTOBER 28th 1880'

The second vessel to hit the pier was the brig *Saffron*, which tore a 200 foot hole through its centre before coming to rest nearby. The *Saffron* had been part of a flotilla of ships which had set out from the Humber, journeying northwards. Around Flamborough Head, the wind increased rapidly to a storm force gale. The fleet was at the mercy of the elements. The *Saffron's* captain made the decision to head back to Hull, but its sails were torn away in the fierce winds and lashing rain. The boat was pulled further and further southwards and nearer to the coast, crashing into the pier in the early hours of the morning. Having lodged against a groyne, the crew bravely sat out the storm until first light when they lowered a ladder and walked to safety. The pier had only just been repaired when it was damaged again on 28 March 1882, the pier head being destroyed along with the saloon above it. The pier was not repaired, but the remaining sections continued in use.

The series of disasters were relentless, and on 20 October 1890, the Grimsby fishing smack *Genesta* hit the pier destroying over half its length, leaving just over 300 feet remaining. The story began at 4 o'clock on Sunday morning when the *Genesta* came aground at Waxholme, near Withernsea. The horrific events were graphically portrayed in the *York Herald.*

The wreck of the Saffron as it smashes into Withernsea Pier.

'When the vessel struck, the third hand was on watch, the captain, Henry Hill, having just gone below after being on deck nearly all the night. Tremendous waves broke over the vessel and the crew had to take to the rigging, this being their only place of safety. Here they remained until 6 o'clock suffering intense agony from the extreme cold, when they were espied by the Coastguard. The Officer shouted at them to keep up their courage, and immediately ran to Withernsea for assistance. The rocket apparatus arrived about 6.30, and was instrumental in landing the crew, with the exception of the captain, who had died owing to the terrible cold, and whose corpse was hanging in the rigging. One who was at the scene of the wreck describes it as one of the most distressing and heartrending scenes ever witnessed on the Withernsea coast ... When rescued the crew were numbed with cold and it was pitiful to see them look up and thank their deliverers.'

The *Genesta* had escaped the ravages of the storm unbroken. It was quickly bought by a group of local businessmen. Before they could protect their purchase, a further storm carried the unmanned vessel up the coast to Withernsea where it crashed into the pier leaving just 300 remaining. Two years later even this was destroyed, when another vessel, the *Henry Parr* (formerly the *Dido*) rammed into it at the height of another storm.

The history of the pier at Withernsea is both tragic, yet inspiring. The two entrance towers have survived all the devastation around them. They are a well-loved landmark in the town, even if many visitors are totally unaware that they once formed a part of a pier. They also act as a memorial to those sailors who perished in the seas around it.

The last pier to be built in Yorkshire was in Hornsea. The town had been attracting a steady stream of visitors for a while and there was hope that, with the coming of the railways, it could turn into a major resort. There was fierce competition between two potential developers who had bought separate parcels of land. Joseph Armytage Wade was a local businessman who ran a large timber company in Hull, whilst Pierre Henri Martin du Gillon hailed from Leeds. For a while, it appeared that the small town might gain two piers but du Gillon's company was declared bankrupt in April 1879 as a result of the cost of court hearings between the two.

With the field now clear, Wade and the Hornsea Pier Company employed Eugenius Birch to design the pier but with only a small amount of capital they were soon in trouble and both designer and contractor were working unpaid. When Bergheim, the contractors, ceased work on the construction a new firm, Fontaine and Co. were brought in to complete the work.

The pier was finally opened to the public in May 1880. With the company now £2,500 in debt, it was immediately placed in the hands of the receivers. Ironically, the pier proved to be a success with visitors, probably becoming the town's main attraction. Its life though, was to be extremely short. The vessel *Earl of Derby* hit the end of the pier during the infamous storm of 28 October in the same year; less than six months after it had opened, the pier head and 120 feet of the rest of the structure had been lost. The remains of the pier were slowly allowed to rot and by 1897 it was declared derelict.

The history of Yorkshire's piers has been littered with tragedy, failure and personal misfortune but also with triumphs, ambition, determination and foresight. In the end, tremendous human engineering skills were at the mercy of the raging sea and howling winds ... and it was nature that won.

Oh, We Do Like to be
Beside the Seaside
1900–1939

The years running up to the outbreak of the Great War were arguably some of the richest in the resorts' history. Visitors flocked to the coast and the coastal towns responded by offering new and more varied sources of amusement and recreation. The largest of the resorts, Scarborough, was still not prepared to sacrifice quality over quantity as it believed resorts such as Blackpool and Morecambe had done. Many of the councillors on the town corporation were from quite strict religious backgrounds and this was evident in their deliberations. Changes did need to be made, however and this was especially evident on its North Bay.

The North Bay of Scarborough had been left virtually undeveloped for many years. An ill-fated attempt to build rock gardens, complete with an assembly hall, capable of seating 3,000 people for concerts, plays, balls and circuses, were a financial disaster, closing after just two years. The development was a solitary one, situated well away from the accommodation and amusements of the South Bay and as such did not attract the visitors it needed to survive. It was also situated on an unstable cliff and eventually the gardens crumbled away into the sea. An attempt to provide a pleasure pier also ended in ruin.

Following the collapse of the rock gardens, the corporation purchased the whole length of the undercliff below Queens Parade as far north as Peasholm Gap. From 1886, the land was drained and landscaped into attractive gardens. A retaining wall and a carriage drive were built to prevent further slippage. The development was named the Clarence Gardens, with a bandstand carefully situated in a

118

protective hollow, but still with views across the bay. Whilst those using the seats around the bandstand paid for the privilege, it was free to those who just wanted to sit on the hill and enjoy the bands and even pierotts. Clarence Gardens was by now a public park.

It was the arrival in the town of Harry W. Smith in January 1897, as the corporation's new Borough Engineer and Surveyor, that was to have such a long-lasting effect on the resort. Formerly the Deputy Engineer in Bournemouth, he was very conscious of the needs not just of visitors but also of local residents and was responsible for the town's first slum clearance and the building of new housing to replace them.

Back in 1889, the Corporation had bought a parcel of land called Great Northstead, which lay between Peasholm Lane and Peasholm Gap. It was renamed Alexandra Field in honour of the Princess of Wales. It was not until late 1907, that work commenced to turn the land, initially, into two bowling greens, tennis courts and an arena with an open stage for performances. At a cost of £4,000, the new works opened on 27 June 1908. Three years later, the area was improved substantially when covered space for performers and an audience of 1,500 was added, together with uncovered seating for the same number. The Floral Hall and Alexandra Gardens were a success and proved that North Bay attractions could be popular and draw visitors from the south of the resort. By 1912, the *Fol-de-Rols,* the well-loved concert party, had moved from Whitby to be the regular performers in the new venue.

Smith was not content just to limit the town's improvements to the North Bay. Scarborough's previous success had been built partly on the attraction of its sea bathing. The days of the bathing machine were almost over and the engineer's next proposal was for an outdoor swimming pool below the Italian formal gardens he was also designing. The pool, which was the first of its kind in the country, was opened by the summer of 1915. Complete with diving boards, water chute, changing facilities and more, it offered visitors everything they could wish for, far in advance of any other English resort. The pool was 350 feet long and 180 feet wide, its water being replenished with every new tide. Behind the pool, the cliff side was landscaped into

The Lake at Peasholm Park.

terraces where a café and rows of 'Beach Bungalows' were provided. A weekly aquatic show was also eventually staged, which in the height of the season attracted large crowds. The Italian gardens featured a lily pond as the centre piece with rose gardens and floral borders surrounding its perimeters. Seats and shelters provided the perfect spot to relax away from the hustle and bustle below.

Perhaps Smith's greatest achievement was the creation of Peasholm Park on a site previously known as Tuckers Field. Situated in the North Bay, which was still largely undeveloped, it was an area of allotments and smallholdings. The blank canvas allowed the engineer's mind to run riot and the outcome was a design for a park in a Japanese style. Work began in December of 1911, finding labour amongst men who would otherwise have been unemployed, something he was to do on several of his projects. Unemployment, especially in the winter months, was rife, a problem common to many resorts whose industry had been almost totally replaced by tourism. The centrepiece of the park was a lake with an island at its centre. A Japanese style bridge linked the two. A boathouse, café and pergolas added to the oriental feel of the park. Amazingly, the first phase of the park was completed within a year and it officially opened on 19 June 1912. It is estimated that the cost of the park was in the region of £2,000.

On the Foreshore, in the South Bay, Catlin's Arcadia had opened in 1909 with room to seat 3,000 visitors to the pierrot shows. This was followed by three picture houses as the craze for the new medium took hold.

The twentieth century witnessed the introduction of new forms of transport. May 1904 saw the construction of a tram system in the town. It ran for four and a half miles and by 1906 was offering a choice of six routes:

- Route 1 - West Pier to Scalby Road via Foreshore Road, Vernon Place, and Falsgrave Road (returning via Prospect Road, Hanover Road, Westborough and Eastborough).
- Route 1A - Aquarium to Scalby Road via Eastborough, Newborough, Westborough and Falsgrave Road (returning via Prospect Road, Hanover Road and Vernon Place).
- Route 2 - Aquarium to Manor Road via Eastborough, Newborough, Westborough, Hanover Road, and Prospect Road (returning via Scalby Road, Falsgrave Road and Vernon Place).
- Route 2A - West Pier to Manor Road via Foreshore Road, Vernon Place, Hanover Road, and Prospect Road (returning via Scalby Road, Falsgrave Road, Westborough, Newborough and Eastborough).
- Route 3 - Railway Station and North Side via Westborough, Aberdeen Walk, Castle Road and North Marine Road.
- Route 4 - South Sands (Marine Drive South Toll House) and North Side via Sandside, Foreshore Road, Vernon Place, Aberdeen Walk, Castle Road, and North Marine Road.

The trams were a success carrying over 22,000 passengers in their first two and a half days of operation. The trams were to continue running until the service, by now owned by the Corporation, closed in September 1931, the United Bus Company being the beneficiaries.

The other great transport innovation was, of course, the motor car. Although work on the town's roads had been carried out in the late nineteenth century, including the removal of the Bar which had narrowed the road between Newborough and Westborough, there was still no easy way of linking the two bays. Consideration had been given to a road hugging the shoreline as early 1881, the first phase of which, the Royal Albert Drive on the North Bay was completed nine years later. The second phase, the Marine Drive linking the two bays, was far more complicated and required a further eighteen years to build. Storms and gales, as well as difficult terrain, played havoc with the build but finally the road was officially opened in August 1908 by Prince Arthur, Duke of Connaught.

The council also purchased all the land on the harbour side of Sandside and constructed a new road there. Whilst it certainly improved the road system, there were some who were sad to see the last of the sailmakers' sheds and lofts disappear.

The final plank in Scarborough's transport policy was the opening of the Excursion Railway Station on Londesborough Road. Especially constructed to handle the high volume of visitors, both day and longer term, arriving and departing by train.

The Edwardian era was also a boom town for Bridlington as a resort. Whilst the majority of the visitors came for the day, many stayed for a week, a fortnight or even longer. By the turn of the century the town could boast over 900 apartments, twelve boarding houses and nine hotels accommodating over 5,000 visitors. The opening of the Spa in 1896 had reduced the number of visitors to the Prince's Parade area. A Hull newspaper wrote in 1897:

'The Prince's Parade, has in previous years, being the great resort of the visitors; but this year, it is feared that someone has made a mess of it. Take the same day last year (not the Whit Monday), the takings at the gate were over £50. At five o'clock on the Bank Holiday, only £10 was taken. The Parade has been

The grand parade for the opening of Scarborough's Marine Drive.

The Princes Parade in Bridlington, the place to be seen. (US Library of Congress)

so deserted that, at one time on Monday evening a stranger supposed that the band was playing for the amusement of the manager and his men. The climax was reached on Sunday night at nine o'clock, when there was only one living creature on the Parade. At the same time there were 4,000 to 5,000 at the Spa.'

The corporation responded in 1904, constructing the Floral Pavilion next to the bandstand in an attempt to revive the Parade's popularity. The cast iron structure was almost fully glazed, with trailing plants cascading from its roof whilst the audience below sat on benches listening to the small orchestra. It was extended in 1907 to incorporate the bandstand. This was quickly followed by the erection of the Grand Pavilion at the north end of the Prince's Parade. The wooden structure could hold almost 2,000 people and was home to a wide variety of entertainment.

The Parade Band continued to play a large part in the entertainment offered, eventually changing their name to the Bridlington Municipal Orchestra in 1907. The orchestra, their conductors and especially the local council met with their fair amount of criticism, not least in letters sent to the local newspaper, the *Bridlington and Quay Gazette*. By 1909, however, the paper reported that the orchestra was 'connected to high calibre ensembles' and that the Bridlington musicians formed a 'high class orchestra'.

Bridlington Corporation also introduced new features to the Parade including a Floral Clock and Staircase. In the evening, the area was illuminated with thousands of fairy lights. *The Bridlington Town Guide* effused over the Parade describing it as:

'at all times a scene of animation and wholesome pleasure'. Especially in the 'magic evening hours when it twinkles with a thousand watching eyes and the moon hangs like a huge Oriental lamp in the sky, spreading its long glories upon the breast of the sea.'

Listening to the orchestra in the Floral Pavilion.

The Spa had not had things all its own way, however. Catastrophe was almost around the corner and on the evening of 20 October 1906, a fire started which quickly engulfed the building. These were the days of horse drawn engines and the brigade were only able to save a part of the building, which included the famous glass dome at one end of the theatre. Quick action was needed and within nine months the new spa was reopened. In 1914, the council leased the building and five years later bought it outright.

The movies made an instant impact on Bridlington. The first 'Cinematography films' were shown at the Grand Pavilion in 1906. By 1909, films were being shown at the New Spa Opera House, the Victoria Rooms, the People's Palace and Field's Oriental Lounge as they all jumped on the bandwagon. The Victorian Temperance Hall became the Picturedrome and was the first dedicated picture house in the town.

Filey, like its two larger neighbours, Scarborough and Bridlington, saw the Edwardian era bring prosperity and good times, especially to the new town. The end of the Boer War saw a sustained period of peace in the country that encouraged the population to enjoy themselves in wholesome recreation. Visitor numbers rose. By the turn of the century, New Filey had developed a reputation for being a stylish resort where families with children were becoming more and more numerous amongst its visitors. They could all be seen promenading through the Crescent Gardens, especially on a Sunday morning after church in their finest clothes. It was still the preserve of the wealthier classes, however, and the family was often accompanied by children's nurses and governesses.

Music was the basis of most of the entertainment on offer in the town with both amateur and professional artistes amongst those performing. The Crescent Gardens still resounded to the sounds of the resident band, but in the Victoria Hall, professional vocalists, often from the London stage, could be heard during the season. The Grand Theatre, on Union Street was opened in 1911 and provided both live entertainment and the new medium, the movies. The building also contained a café and lecture room.

OH, WE DO LIKE TO BE BESIDE THE SEASIDE

By 1890, Whitby had begun to evolve into a resort. *Baines Directory* of that year listed 168 lodging house keepers, fifty-four hotels and inns as well as pleasure boat owners, fossil and mineral shops and other accoutrements of any self-respecting resort. The town had also become a centre for artists and photographers. At the same time, however, the directory also recorded seventy-five master mariners and fourteen ship owners, together with ship and boat builders. Whitby was still in a state of transition and although its traditional occupations including fishing were in decline, they still played a large part in the town's economy.

By the start of the twentieth century, the town was very much one of two halves, the new developments for visitors on the West Cliff,

Whitby's historic abbey has been a magnet for visitors to the former port for many years. (US Library of Congress)

127

Whitby Abbey. (US Library of Congress)

whilst Old Whitby, with its seafaring and fishing connections retained
its original character. It was this evocative picture that Whitby was
keen to portray.

The fishing quarter was promoted as somewhere the visitor would
choose to spend time. It was romanticised in the paintings of Whitby
artists and those of the surrounding colonies at Staithes and Robin
Hood's Bay, together with the photographs of Frank Meadow Sutcliffe.
He earned his living taking portraits of the wealthy and middle classes,
at the same time as producing his now famous images of local
fishermen and towns people, together with seascapes and townscapes
highlighting the towns historic past.

The Yorkshire Coast; Its Advantages and Attractions, published on
behalf of the North Eastern Railway in 1904, emphasised Whitby's
'ancient and picturesque character'. This was not the whole truth,
however, as the Old Town was riddled with slum housing, dirt and
squalor.

Whatever the reason for coming to the town, the growing number of visitors had to be accommodated, fed and entertained. The West Cliff Saloon had opened in 1880, offering a varied programme of music and plays, whilst on the Promenade musicians played throughout the summer. The Spa was purchased by the Urban District Council in 1915 and the Floral Pavilion was eventually built next door.

Even the smaller resorts began to provide new entertainment. Redcar opened its new Palace of Varieties in April 1913. Seating 946 people, a twenty feet wide stage and several dressing rooms by the end of the year, this theatre too, was screening films. Hornsea saw the building of its Floral Hall in 1913 on land at the cliff edge, north of

Whitby Harbour was and still is, a popular place for visitors to discover. (US Library of Congress)

Marine Drive. The land was originally landscaped with bandstand, seats and flowerbeds. Named the Promenade Gardens, it was subject to coastal erosion before the construction of a sea wall and promenade stabilised the project. The hall was the venue for most of the resort's entertainment.

A large hotel, the Hornsea Imperial Hydro, was opened in the Summer of 1913 in an attempt to attract a different clientele to the town. Grandly appointed in mahogany panelling and containing Turkish baths, an indoor swimming pool, theatre and a ballroom, the hotel was only in operation for a year, before being commandeered at the start of the Great War. It was not to open again for thirty years.

The improvements at all these coastal towns in the years before 1914 illustrates the ambition they all shared. They were anticipating the significant growth of the previous few years to continue. The outbreak of the First World War in that year stopped them in their tracks. Not only was the war to change these resorts, but for the millions who survived the killing fields of Europe, their world and their individual lives would be changed for ever.

Whilst the start of the war did not necessarily impact immediately on the resorts – indeed the season had been progressing well – one event on 16 December 1914 brought the conflict to the streets and homes of families in Yorkshire as they were preparing for Christmas. At just after eight o'clock in the morning, the German battleships *Derrflinger* and *Von der Tann* emerged from the mist off Scarborough and bombarded the town for over thirty minutes. The next day, *The Yorkshire Post* reported that:

'Several prominent buildings including the Parish Church, St Martin's Church, and the Grand Hotel were damaged and there was considerable loss of life. Fifteen people are reported to have been killed and many injured.'

It is estimated that 500 shells rained down on the town, thirty-six of them on the Grand Hotel alone, which cost over £13,000 to repair.

A resident of Dean Road described the scene:

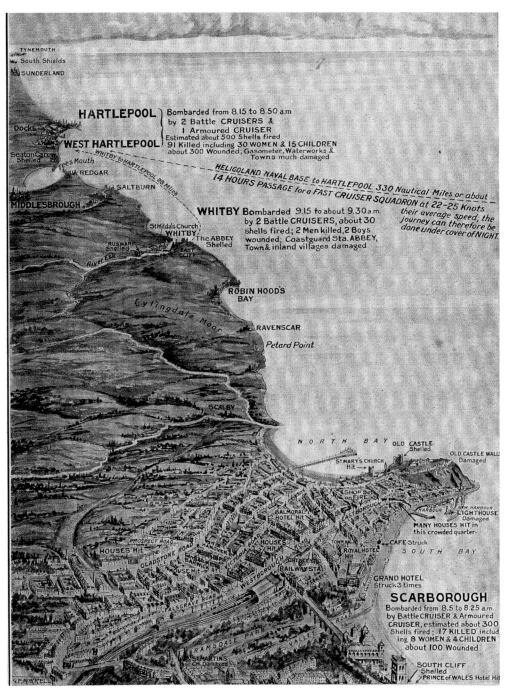

The map shows the German warships devastating progress up the east coast of England.

Kingscliffe Camp Offices damaged in the German Bombardment. The buildings overlooked the South Bay. (The Illustrated London War News)

'I heard a dull boom, then a peculiar whizzing sound followed almost immediately by an ear splitting crack. This was clearly no thunder. I went to the bath room and through the window I saw a rapid succession of vivid flashes in the offing. It was nearly daylight and there was a mist over the water. The flashes appeared to be like so many balls of fire over the sea. I saw a house in Mayfield Avenue some 300 yards away, across an open space, struck by a shell. First the roof quivered and then the slates flew in all directions. Afterwards the bricks of the walls began tumbling down.'

A house in Lonsdale Road, badly damaged in the same attack. (The Illustrated London War News)

The loss of life which caused most outrage, however, was that at 2, Wykeham Street, home to the Bennett family and several paying guests. Those killed were Johanna Bennett (58), Albert Bennett (22), John Ward (10) and George James Barnes (5). In total, seventeen people lost their lives in Scarborough that day.

During the attack, an exodus began, with residents, often partially dressed, abandoning their homes and businesses and making for the railway station, escaping to nearby Hull and York or further inland to the West Riding. Much of the panic centred around the fear that the attack was a precursor to an invasion. Nearby troops took up positions defending the beach, with reinforcements being sent from York. When the assault did not happen, many inhabitants came back the next day, with some hardy souls even returning later that same evening.

Following their attack on Scarborough, the *Derrflinger* and *Von der Tann* turned their attentions on Whitby. The damage was lighter than at Scarborough but the town still suffered damage to forty properties with 200 shells being fired in just ten minutes. The signalling and Coastguard stations were destroyed. Three people were killed.

The attacks on the soft targets of Scarborough and Whitby together with the bombardment of Hartlepool on the same day, allowed more than 100 enemy mines to be laid between Filey and Flamborough Head. During the remainder of the war, these would play havoc with local shipping with the loss of many boats and lives. Indeed, Scarborough was to be attacked again in September 1917, when a submarine surfaced and fired thirty shells killing three people. The German navy had been keen to exploit the vulnerability of much of the relatively unguarded east coast. It had ignored the accepted protocols and conventions of the day, directly attacking civilians in their homes. The *Scarborough Mercury* was indignant It captured the feelings of Scarborough at the time. They wrote:

'The Germans must pay and every penny. We are assured by the allies that the war will not terminate until the Germans are on their knees and prepared to accept the terms decided upon by the allies.'

134

The British government wasted no time in utilising the attacks for propaganda purposes. A string of recruitment posters was issued demanding that the population should 'REMEMBER SCARBOROUGH'. It was estimated each poster raised 1,000 extra men.

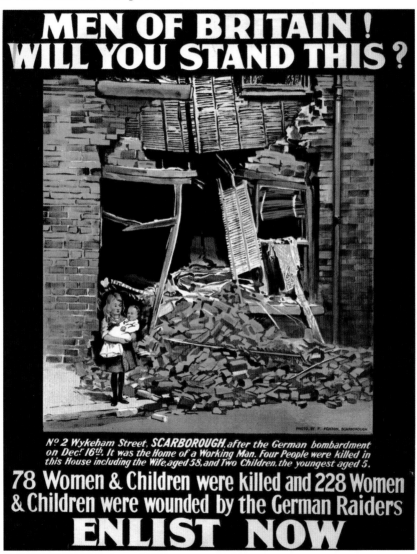

The bombardment of Scarborough was swiftly used in propaganda posters. It was estimated that each poster was worth one thousand extra recruits.

BESIDE THE SEASIDE

The 1914 attack quickly began to fade in the population's memory as vast amounts of casualties began to be reported from France, Belgium and Gallipoli. Here, the dead were measured in their thousands and the public began to accept that this was a war like none before.

Britain had gone to war in the middle of the holiday season. It was not until the next season that its full impact was noticed. An article in the *Yorkshire Weekly Post*, specifically about Bridlington, could have been true of any of the major east coast resorts at the time. The numbers of visitors were down significantly and the town appeared strangely deserted:

> 'Where large preparations have been made for the accommodation of a crowd, the absence of a crowd always give a place a more or less deserted feeling than a ball room with only three couples dancing with a strangely anti-festive look. So, where big promenades on which, at this time of the year one is in the habit of seeing thousands, have a strangely deserted appearance when only hundreds are to be seen.'

Hotels and boarding houses were used for military purposes and for the billeting of troops. Parts of the beaches were used for training exercises. Minesweepers could be observed operating just off shore at the same time as local boats were offering fishing trips to visitors:

> 'Despite the fact that the Germans believe that the ocean is occupied entirely by their mines and submarines, one was invited in the usual manner of peace times to go fishing, or sailing. As you stepped down to the pier, the invitation was issued in the usual informal way and the bay was studded with sails, as if to give the doubters confidence. True, the "Frenchman" (Pleasure Steamer) was not running, but then one must remember that every Frenchman has other work to do than that of cruising about for pleasure.'

The war years were difficult for the east coast resorts. Yes, visitors did come, but not in the numbers of previous years; day trippers were almost non-existent. Restrictions were placed on hotel advertising and most of their male staff were away fighting at the front. Public gardens continued to be tended and even if buildings were not maintained in the same careful way as before, they survived. As the 1915 article concluded, albeit without the knowledge that the war would last a further three years:

'with the sun shining brilliantly upon the white cliffs and gleaming out against the blue of sea and sky, with everything at normal, and with plums three halfpence a pound less than at Morecambe, surely there is nothing to keep the visitors away. As the fisherman says: "It's them awful gales as gets about what spoils things for us."'

When peace came with the signing of the armistice in 1918, people eventually began to return to the coast in increasing numbers. By 1921, the Corporation at Scarborough had appointed a manager to oversee events in Peasholm Park and the South Bay Swimming Pool which had opened at the height of the war in 1915. The castle and the headland around it were also taken back into council hands having been used in the war years for soldier training, It now belongs to English Heritage.

Harry Smith's plans for Scarborough had largely been put on hold during the war. Following the cessation of hostilities and backed by Alderman Sit Meredith Whittaker, they were firmly back on the table. The Council purchased outright the whole of the Northstead Estate in 1921, eventually allowing for the extension of Peasholm Park and the creation of the Northstead Manor Gardens. Within three years, Wilson's Wood had been transformed into the Glen, a woodland walk, now featuring streams waterfalls and a lily pond. Major improvements to Peasholm Park followed. A pagoda on the island with a waterfall cascading down below it, a miniature golf course and a bandstand on the lake were just some of the new features.

In 1925, the corporation extended the promenade northwards and the Corner Café complex was opened at a cost of £32,000; including

The pagoda and waterfall on the island at Peasholm Park.

a restaurant and dance/concert hall, it was a major investment. Two more projects followed soon on its heels. The first was the construction of a miniature railway running from Peasholm Park to Scalby Mills. Running for just short of one mile, the line was twenty inch gauge. The line opened on 23 May 1931 when the locomotive, *Neptune*, was officially handed over to the Mayor of Scarborough, Alderman Whitehead with a short presentation speech:

'On behalf of the National Union of Drivers, Engineers and others, I have to present you, the first driver of the North Bay Railway Engine, with your insignia of office, your oil can and your "sweat rag".'

The mayor was presented with a peaked cap, an oil can (adorned with a blue ribbon), and a rag, before driving the train from Peasholm Station non-stop to Scalby Mills, at which point the engine was transferred to the other end of the train for the return journey. The first locomotive was the *Neptune* followed shortly after by the *Triton*. Altogether six engines have operated on the railway during its eighty years existence.

Scarborough's Open Air Theatre was opened by the Lord Mayor of London in Northstead Manor Gardens in 1932, with audiences eager to see *Merrie England*, the first production staged in such a glorious venue. The Mayor was reputed to have said:

'The setting is ideal and constitutes a wonderful tribute to the imagination of whoever realised the possibilities to be derived from this particular part of the park, and also to the engineers who carried out the necessary embellishments and alterations which provide such a picturesque stage and background and also such splendid accommodation.'

The theatre itself was built on the site of Hodgson's Slack, which was a natural amphitheatre. The stage was set on an island in the middle of a lake with fixed seating for the audience opposite. It was set out in five blocks with 5,876 seats, and the balance was made up with deck

139

Musicals performed at the Open Air Theatre often featured up to two hundred performers.

chairs. The amphitheatre drew thousands each night, offering theatrical productions and lavish musicals on a scale that few of today's producers can even hope for, with casts of over 200 actors and singers. It enjoyed an amazing history with regular sell out events by Scarborough Operatic Society, who leased the theatre from the corporation. Musicals such as *The King and I, Annie Get Your Gun* and *Hiawatha*, which saw native American warriors in canoes paddling on to the football pitch sized stage. Shows were performed during the summer season, two performances being held each week.

After the retirement of Harry Smith in 1933, new work on the North Bay was vastly reduced, the only major pre-war work being the construction of the North Bay Bathing Pool at a cost of £30,000. The complex contained a pool which was heated to sixty-eight degrees.

Much of the work undertaken in the North Bay preserved its character of being less commercialised and more natural that its southern neighbour, a distinction that to some extent holds true today. On the South Bay, the Spa had been somewhat neglected during the war. By 1927, its centenary year, it had been transformed; a new ballroom had been built with the rest of the building being fully refurbished. The *Centenary Souvenir Booklet* produced that year proclaimed that the spa was 'the most lustrous leisure-place in the country' and that the time when 'the hush of twilight was on it from October till April' and 'that period of placid is now ended. A new era has dawned'. This period coincided with the tenure as conductor of the Spa orchestra of Alick Maclean, under whom they regained their former reputation.

If the Spa was still aimed at the town's upmarket visitors, the foreshore continued to cater for the day visitor and those seeking a good time. Here, Catlin ruled the roost, with the Arcadia theatre, built in 1909 offering Pierrot shows together with the Olympia Picture Palace. This was followed by nearby Palladium Picture House, which,

The North Bay Bathing Pool looking across to Castle Hill.

when opened in 1914, was one of the most glamorous cinemas in the country. Catlin was a showman and when he opened the Futurist Super Cinema on the site of the old Arcadia, it had his trademarks all over it. Built by Frank Tugwell, a locally renowned architect, it was designed to be used for both live performances, often by its own resident orchestra, and for the showing of silent films. The films with orchestral and theatre organ accompaniment, were shown every evening and on several afternoons, all through the year. The auditorium featured upholstered seating for 3,000 and an American Soda Fountain and Ice Cream Saloon was one of the cinema's most popular features. As the moving image became more popular than live performance, several more cinemas sprang up around the town culminating in the opening of the Odeon Cinema in 1936.

The other major change on the South Bay was at the former aquarium. By the 1920s, the attraction was again in financial difficulties forcing the council to take it into their control in 1925. Renamed 'Gala Land' it offered 'Melody, Mirth and Merriment' and was open until eleven in the evening. The venue became famous for its use of all-female bands.

By the outbreak of the Second World War, Scarborough was able to offer entertainment that appealed to all of its visitors, albeit still in their own carefully designated areas. Long gone were the days when it catered only for the select few. As Adman's report into the future development of Scarborough was to note, nowhere else 'was better able to entertain all classes'.

Bridlington's progress had also been put on hold during the Great War. As in Scarborough, it was something the council were quick to address. Having bought the Spa in 1919, they replaced the last of the original building in 1925 with the new Spa Royal Hall. The author of the 1929 *Bridlington Guide* was inspired to write:

'built only three years ago at a cost of £50,000. Here, more than 4,000 people can be entertained simultaneously, the immense dance floor being surrounded by a deep terrace, and spacious balconies above giving a perfect view to a great number of

Gala Land, the home of 'Melody, Mirth and Merriment'.

onlookers. The Hall itself is a beautiful building with a stained glass dome.'

In a case of history repeating itself this new building was badly affected by fire in January 1932. The theatre was able to reopen at Easter of that year and amazingly the new Royal Hall was rebuilt in just fifty-five days. Plays and variety shows were held in the theatre whilst dancing was the mainstay of the hall. The most famous of the

Spa's musical directors was Herman Darewski, who held the post extremely successfully for ten years during the period 1923-39. The Minsk-born conductor's name became synonymous with the resort, drawing in dancers from far and wide. The Spa became one of the north's most popular music venues.

More new buildings followed. The Floral Hall opened in 1921 but was burned down two years later. The next venture, the Coliseum, opened in 1922 on the Promenade. Within two years, it had changed its name to the Winter Gardens. The opening was reported in the *Bridlington Free Press*.

'The magnificent new centre of amusement, The Coliseum, which is situated on the Promenade, Bridlington, was opened in the presence of a large company on Easter Monday afternoon by the Mayor of the Borough …

'A capital pictorial entertainment followed a nicely diversified programme of films, of both an amusing and instructive character, being shown. There were some grand animal pictures, whilst one of much educational value described "How the telephone speaks."

'The chief attraction, however, was the screen version of the stage success, The Sign on the Door, featuring Norma Talmadge, the thrilling picture drama riveting the attention of the large audience from start to finish.'

Despite being sold in 1924, the Winter Gardens was a popular attraction. The *Ward Lock Guide 1927/28* stated that it was 'One of the finest entertainment halls in the district', containing 'an up-to-date theatre and picture hall, a spacious ballroom, café and roof café'.

On the Prince's Parade, the Grand Pavilion was demolished in 1936. It was replaced by the new Grand Pavilion on Victoria Terrace Gardens. The stylish white building was of modern design and faced onto the Promenade.

Bridlington Corporation was also determined to protect its heritage and rural spaces. It purchased Sewerby Hall and Park in 1934 followed by the Danes Dyke Estate the year after. It subsequently acquired Flamborough Head in 1939. The hall, built in 1714, was opened to the public on 1 June 1938 by aviator Amy Johnson. According to the 1939 *Guide*, the Park (as it was described) was 'Bridlington's Glorious Beauty Spot' with 'Beautiful Old World and Ornamental Gardens'. Visitor facilities included a nine-hole golf course, crown green bowling and putting greens, croquet lawn, archery butts and an aviary. A restaurant and café were open by this date.

The town had also been keen to improve its road system in order to satisfy the growing number of visitors, travelling firstly by char-a-banc, motor coach and subsequently by private car. Promenades were also extended with the building of the Princess Mary Promenade and North Marine Drive.

Bridlington was also at the vanguard of a new type of holiday. Over the last 200 years, visitors had stayed in inns, hotels, boarding houses and apartments. A new generation of traveller required more freedom, less restrictions and, just as importantly, cheaper holidays. The days of visitors coming for the 'Season' were also gone, with a week or a fortnight the norm. Camping and self-catering accommodation was becoming more and more popular. By 1938, it was estimated that over 500,000 people took an annual camping holiday. Campsites could be found at Danes Dyke and in Sewerby Village.

Another campsite was recorded at Limekiln Lane in the south of the town around 1920. Several years later, tents and bungalows were being joined by bus bodies, converted railway carriages, trailers and caravans. The site continues to exist to this day. Single men, couples and families could all be seen enjoying an alfresco breakfast of bacon and eggs by the sea.

Smaller scale development continued in Whitby with the opening of the Coliseum offering a diet of music and variety. Whitby had always been a popular spot for concert parties and pierrots, probably the first of whom were George Royal's Imps who moved to the east coast from Blackpool. They eventually transferred to Scarborough under the name the Fol-de-Rols. The Gay Cadets amused visitors down on the beach between 1911 and 1916, even bringing their own

Caravan and camping became more and more popular as visitors turned to holidays outdoors.

stage with them, transferring the whole set to Battery Place each evening for another show. The Bouquets concert party became a regular fixture at the Spa Theatre from the 1920s for over forty years.

During the 1930s, new hotels began to open, the Monk's Haven and Morningside amongst them. Often the new hotels were boarding houses or small hotels that were joined together to create larger establishments.

Even the smaller resort of Redcar was still looking to improve its facilities. The New Pavilion was built in 1928 over what had been the entrance to Coatham Pier. It was roofed entirely in glass, seated up to 800 and was used as a music hall and theatre. It was eventually turned into a cinema.

Down the coast, gardens continued to be a vital ingredient in Filey's leisure facilities throughout the 1920s and '30s. A small orchestra played throughout the season for both listening and dancing. Before a sun lounge was built, there was a small but extremely popular area for outdoor dancing. By 1939, there was open air dancing on Monday, Wednesday and Saturday to an orchestra of seven musicians.

Visitors' expectations and tastes were changing, however. In response, the Southdene Pavilion opened as a dance hall in 1935. A stage was eventually added and shows were performed regularly throughout the season. The year 1937 saw concert parties presenting shows with the evocative titles; Holiday Fair, Gala Revels, Kit-Kat Kits and Vivacity amongst others, each party performing for just one week.

The 1930s were a boom time for Filey. Development commenced at nearby Primrose Valley, initially for camping but as the use of private motor cars grew this expanded into other forms of accommodation and housing for permanent residents. Entrepreneur Billy Butlin bought 120 acres of land at nearby Hunmanby Gap for the sum of £12,000, a considerable amount of money at the time. Construction of his latest holiday camp started the year after. Butlin had made his money with a series of amusement parks. His idea for the holiday camp came after a disappointing childhood holiday. He and his parents had been locked out of their bedroom from after breakfast until teatime, as was the standard practice in boarding houses at the time. He believed that families should have access to their rooms at any time. His first camp was opened in Skegness in 1936, followed by a second in Clacton two years later. His third camp was to become synonymous with Filey over a period of forty-four years. It might never have been built, however, as shortly into its construction the country was yet again rocked by the outbreak of war. This time, Yorkshire's seaside resorts were to be even more seriously affected than before.

Difficult Years
1939–1950

The outbreak of the Great War had caught the Yorkshire resorts by surprise. Indeed, the 1914 season had been in full swing, with plans for the next year already in place. With the Second World War, it was different. The country had been dreading but anticipating its entry into the conflict for many long months. Prior to the signing of the Munich Agreement in September 1938, arrangements were well advanced to deal with the outbreak of war. Gas masks were already being delivered to the county and distributed to the public. On 1 September the following year, when Germany invaded Poland, 5,000 child evacuees from Hull immediately found themselves in Scarborough, arriving at Londesborough Excursion Station. Nearly 20,000 more children with some adults from Hull and the north east arrived in the next few days with more billeted to Bridlington, Filey and the surrounding areas shortly afterwards. Places more adept at welcoming streams of eager visitors had to then deal with an influx of a different type.

The children arrived, usually on a council charted train, armed with a gas mask, identity card and a case packed in line with government instructions: The Yorkshire coast had been chosen as suitable for evacuees not just because it was deemed a relatively safe area, but because the resort towns had a large capacity of unused accommodation. In fact, many residents had temporarily moved away to stay with family in other parts of the country. Some hotels agreed to accept a quota of evacuees, although in the early stages of the war some holiday visitors continued to arrive at the resort, though in greatly reduced numbers. With the German army occupied in eastern Europe, the threatened onslaught did not occur and gradually many of the evacuees drifted home. By April of the next year over 6,000 had left Scarborough alone.

The declaration of war saw the immediate closure of all places of entertainment and a total blackout at night enforced. The latter was to remain in force for the duration. Within a few days, many of the cinemas had reopened, followed by Scarborough's Olympia Ballroom, albeit with the restriction that dancers would be refused admission without a gas mask. The Pavilion Hotel even applied for and received an extension to its licence allowing the bars to open until midnight. Across the resorts, many of the venues reopened, including both Scarborough and Bridlington Spas. This proved to be a very temporary measure but nevertheless many visitors were accommodated over the Christmas period in 1939, including over 4,000 in Scarborough. An interesting evening must have been enjoyed at the Grand Hotel on 15 December when a dish of Macon and Eggs was served. The new dish of Macon was made from mutton and, as an alternative to bacon, proved reasonably popular!

Scarborough, even went as far as producing its 1940 *Guide*. The Pavilion Hotel was offering reduced wartime rates from 12 shillings per day complete with dancing, daily concerts and tennis courts. The Blincoln Boarding House on Westborough, however, announced that 'Food will be as good and plentiful as possible under rationing conditions'; all from just over two pounds per week. Eventually, a law was passed that meals served in hotels and restaurants 'must not cost over five shillings per customer, must not be of more than three courses, and at most one course could contain meat, fish or poultry'.

In Filey, Billy Butlin proved that a wily businessman could be successful whatever the situation. In a meeting with Hore-Belisha, the Minister for War, he negotiated a deal whereby the government would finance the finishing of the camp and, after using it during the war, he (Butlin) would buy it back at sixty per cent of its value. RAF Hunmanby Moor became home to 6,000 military personnel including at one stage over 5,000 West Indian recruits. A long way from their Caribbean homes, they trained as flight and motor mechanics, radio technicians, cooks and admin clerks.

As the war progressed, more and more hotels and boarding houses were requisitioned by the government for the billeting of troops and

After the Second World War, the beaches and cliffs were littered with sea defences, pillboxes and armaments. (Adobe Images)

other military uses. Scarborough Castle became an RAF direction finding station. The coastal resorts gradually took on the appearance of a cross between a military fortress and a war zone. This was especially evident following the disaster of Dunkirk, when a German invasion as far north as Yorkshire seemed a real possibility. Beaches were closed, barbed wire, pillboxes and concrete anti-tank defences were erected.

Mines were laid both on the beach and out to sea including in the harbour at Scarborough, the detonation device for which was in a pillbox at the foot of Blands Cliff, disguised as an ice cream kiosk. Soldiers and sometimes volunteers, as was the case in Redcar, guarded the roads leading to the promenades and foreshores. Saltburn and Redcar Piers were once again sectioned to prevent their use by the enemy. Many of the entertainment venues that had previously reopened were now closed down once again.

DIFFICULT YEARS

3 February 1940 saw Whitby make history, when the first German plane to crash on English soil during the war did so near a farm on the outskirts of the town. The Heinkel III bomber had been badly damaged in a firefight with three British Hurricanes led by Lieutenant Peter Townsend (later to be more famous for his relationship with Princess Margaret).

It was from the air that the major threat to the coastal towns came. Bridlington, especially the harbour, was a target in its own right. It also happened to be a suitable point to offload any bombs leftover from numerous raids on the city of Hull. The northern port was a gateway to the world and as such was a major target. Over 85,000 houses were damaged or destroyed and 1,200 people killed.

The 11 July 1940 saw five people killed in Bridlington when bombs fell on Prince Street and Hilderthorpe Road. August saw Prince Street hit twice more, destroying the Britannia Hotel amongst several other buildings. Boats were damaged in the harbour. Thursday 15 August was one the most important days of the whole Battle of Britain for the north-east area, with raids up and down its entire length. The German plan had been to overwhelm the country's entire air defence system. The attack met with stern opposition, however, with over seventy-five enemy planes destroyed.

Scarborough had been classified as a military area and as such was a target for lone German planes. In August 1940, an eight-year-old boy was killed when a plane attacked the gasworks in Seamer Road. After machine gunning six workers at the site, it proceeded to drop four bombs. The boy, Ernest Gates, ran straight into the blast and was instantly killed. An attack on 10 October created a crater sixty feet wide and thirty feet deep. Several houses were destroyed and over 500 damaged. Casualties would have been much higher, if a large number of people had not been attending a Spitfire Dance at the Olympia Ballroom on the Foreshore.

The town's worst raid was on 18 March 1941, when planes deluged the resort for several hours with high explosive bombs, parachute mines and incendiary devices. Over 1,300 buildings were damaged with the loss of twenty-eight lives. In one household, five people were killed instantly when a bomb landed in their front room whilst they were sitting around the fire. The Queen's Hotel was so badly damaged that it was never repaired and was demolished in 1948. Many of Scarborough's buildings were alight and although fire engines from around the north rushed to the town, a large proportion were lost. Amazingly, only one fireman was killed. As a result of the raid, over 1,500 public air raid shelters and fifty static water tanks were added to the town's streets.

None of the county's coastal towns were immune from attacks. Filey, Whitby and Saltburn, as well as the more southern resorts of the East Riding suffered. It is hardly surprising that no one wanted to visit the area.

As the war progressed, air raids diminished and the expected invasion had not been forthcoming. Some restrictions were lifted or relaxed. April 1942 saw the beach on Scarborough's South Bay being reopened during daylight hours, with the North Bay reopening for the summer in June the following year. Swimming in the sea was still prohibited though, due to the danger of mines. Filey continued to be filled with troops in its role as a training base. September 1944 saw the easing of blackout restrictions and by Christmas of that year, cars could once again use their full headlights. By February 1945, pleasure craft were operating up to two and a half miles offshore.

The war in Europe ended on 8 May 1945. The resorts had been left battered and bruised. Many of the hotels used as billets for soldiers had suffered from vandalism and neglect, as had the former grand places of entertainment. They were in need of considerable repair and renovation. Whilst the resorts threw themselves into the work almost immediately, they also had to deal with a severe shortage of housing and destroyed public buildings.

Numerous hotels had to wait months before the troops finally left and repairs could begin. In Scarborough, the Balmoral was the first to reopen in March 1945. Others were months and even years before they were once again taking paying guests. Over in Bridlington, the Expanse and Alexandra Hotels remained closed until 1948 and 1949 respectively. Despite many of the hotels and boarding houses still being requisitioned, over 750,000 people stayed in Scarborough in the four months from June 1945. To assist with the shortage of accommodation, local councils turned to small householders who opened up their homes to visitors for the first time.

Over 80,000 people visited the Open Air Theatre when the Operatic Society revived 'Merrie England'. 100,000 attended the orchestral concerts on the Spa with Neale Kelley and his Orchestra reopening the attraction for the first time since 1939. Bridlington too, was enjoying a successful period with the council extending the season due to the high number of visitors. The Spa Royal Hall and the Grand Pavilion reopened in time for the 1946 season hosting Ceres Harper and his New Dance Orchestra together with a summer review *Gaiety Fayre* respectively.

At Whitby, the story was the same, with the season being extended to meet the massive demand. All available accommodation was quickly sold out. Whilst there were no bathing facilities available, the cliff lift was running, allowing easy access to the promenade. Dancing at the Spa and celebrity concerts were held throughout the season.

Whilst the resorts initial needs began to be met, labour and building materials were in short supply and financial resources extremely stretched. It was several years before any major works, essential repairs and improvements could be undertaken. Times were difficult at the seaside, but on the horizon was the last golden period that they were to enjoy.

Changing Times
1950–2000

It was the early 1950s before anything like normality returned to the holiday resorts. Although most hotels and boarding houses had been returned to their owners by the military by 1947, it was several more years before numbers reached their pre-war levels, heralding a 'decade of plenty' for the Yorkshire coast.

The 1950s were the halcyon days of the English seaside resort before the development of the cheap package holiday tempted visitors further afield. Holidays with pay were now enforced by law and many workers could afford a holiday week at the coast. Most visitors stayed in small guest houses, or in holiday camps and caravan parks. A new innovation, 'Holiday Flats', first made their introduction around 1955. The beaches at Scarborough, Bridlington and Filey would be full to capacity on bustling summer bank holidays, a swarming mass of holidaymakers intent on enjoying every minute of their stay. The smaller resorts from Redcar to Withernsea were also filled with trippers escaping the industrial heartlands of Middlesbrough and Hull.

Paul Fenton recalled his annual family holiday to Scarborough:

'Every year our next door neighbours, Mr and Mrs Swain, very kindly filled two small containers with sixpences; when the containers were full you pressed the tiny lever on the side and the lid popped off so you could get at the money. A whole pounds worth each! We were well off

'Great excitement as we loaded my aunt and uncle's tiny Ford Popular; not such a straight forward journey then; no motorways and almost non-existent dual carriageways.

'As we approached Scarborough we imagined we could see

The Three B's – Bright, Breezy and Bracing Bridlington

by the colour of the sky that we were near the sea. The sky was always blue; no rain on holiday in those days. We found our way to our private hotel. We thought it was really posh! A good breakfast every morning and dinner (with 3 courses!) in the evening.

'The first day we headed straight for the shop to buy new buckets and spades (the ones we had from last year never lasted the full year) and paper flags, depicting the individual 4 nations of the UK, for our sandcastles. Mornings were usually spent on the beach. No matter how hard we tried we could never get the sea to fill the moats properly, even with the addition of bucket loads of extra water.

'Around midday we would go to a café for cups of tea and sandwiches. Having a sweet tooth, I almost invariably bought a knickerbocker glory with my holiday money. The joy of using the long spoon to get at the different layers of ice cream, jelly and fruit, Heaven!

'Afternoons were usually spent walking; going to the various gardens, the castle, etc. If it was really hot, it was the beach again. When we were older, on one occasion, we went to the pictures (cinema) A real treat!

'The Grand Hotel, at that time, was very posh, but my dad, being my dad and despite my mum's protestations, insisted on going in for a look. As usual he was successful in bluffing his way to the reception to ask for details. He came out with a smile on his face declaring that the carpet pile was so thick it reached to his knees resulting in one of the hotel staff asking if he'd lost his legs in the war.'

In Scarborough, there was little in council coffers for massive new attractions and entertainment venues. Under the inspirational leadership of Entertainments Manager, George Horrocks, smaller projects aimed at children and families were developed. Back in 1927, Horrocks had been the driving force behind the introduction of the miniature mock naval battle on the lake in Peasholm Park. During the war, the boats rotted away in storage, so Horrrocks had a completely new set flotilla to be constructed allowing the Battle of the River Plate to be fought twice weekly to this day. Around 1960, aircraft were added to the display. These days there is far less emphasis on fighting battles from actual wars, just between friends and enemies! The attraction is still as popular as ever.

CHANGING TIMES

A second introduction that Horrocks made was the *Hispaniola*. The one quarter sale replica of an eighteenth century schooner was launched in June 1949 and decorated as a pirate ship. It sailed on Scarborough Mere for over forty years bringing joy to countless children. Treasure was hidden on a small island in the mere and the 'pirates' were allowed to search for the hidden doubloons; a swashbuckling adventure worthy of a Hollywood film. The *Hispaniola* was out of service for over twenty years but now sails Scarborough's South Bay throughout the summer.

The third and largest project was the illuminated tree walk in Peasholm Park. Costing over £7,000, the attraction opened in 1953. The pathways snaking around the island were illuminated by thousands of fairy lights and models and tableaux taken from children's fairy tales and other books. 'It was magical, if not a bit scary in the dark. The lights were used to great effect.'

Another venture opened at the same time was the Space Ship ride situated on the foreshore below the Grand Hotel. It was named *Anastasia* at an opening ceremony by Frances Day, the American actress and singer. After visiting the Tree Walk she said that she had 'never seen such enchantment'. The Whitsuntide holiday of 1953 brought in record receipts totalling £4,000. The increase was largely due to the new family friendly attractions.

The 1953 season saw all the resorts back to their best with a wide variety of entertainment and attractions on offer. 'Zahla,' the 'blindfold intuitionist and musical enigma at the piano' and Stan Aces 'magical comedian and card manipulator' entertaining at the Floral Pavilion in Bridlington. At the Grand Pavilion, the reviews, *Burlington Follies* and *Gayety Fayre* were performed whilst at Scarborough's Arcadia (formerly the Palladium Picture House), similar fayre was available in *Catlin's Showtime*. The Reginald King Orchestra and Jay Langham's Dance Orchestra performed at Whitby Spa.

The open-air theatre in Northstead Manor Gardens was revived from 1945. By the 1950s out had gone operetta and in were the musicals. The 1953 season production was *Annie Get Your Gun* following on from a record breaking run of the *Desert Song* when over

157

'Magical and enchanting'.

160,000 people from all over the north of England saw the production. It was Britain's largest theatre with a capacity of almost 9,000.

The year 1957 saw the Futurist Cinema on Scarborough's Foreshore being converted for live theatre. The old theatre organ was removed and a proscenium added. It became a popular venue for shows and concerts featuring well known acts as well as for summer seasons.

Scarborough Spa was slower to recover from the war. Although it reopened at Whitsuntide in 1945, it had been badly damaged and neglected over the previous five years. In 1953, the Spa Company sold the footbridge to the council who promptly abolished the one penny charge. It was not until November 1957 that they also bought the Spa outright and the complex was once again in council hands. Fees to the promenade and Spa grounds were also quickly ended. Minor repairs and renovations were undertaken, but it was to be many years before the building received the attention it badly needed.

Bridlington Spa appeared to recover somewhat quicker and the 1953 season found Ceres Harper and his New Dance Orchestra performing in the Royal Hall whilst the Court Players were in repertory at the Spa Theatre.

In Filey, Butlin's Holiday Camp was the perfect barometer of the nation's love of the English seaside holiday. Following the war, half the camp was handed back to Billy Butlin and with the help of over 400 servicemen, the camp partially reopened on 2 June of that year. It initially accommodated 1,500 visitors but by the end of the season the capacity had risen to 5,000. Eventually this figure increased to 11,000.

'We're going to spend a holiday,
We've worked and saved all year,
We've put our worries on the shelf,
We haven't got a care,
We've caught a train, an early one,
To Filey, by the sea,
And now we're here at Butlin's
That's the place for you and me.'

The camp's own railway station had opened in 1947. A road train would meet the visitors and transport them through a tunnel under the main road to the reception building. It was estimated that in the early 1950s, up to half of the visitors arrived this way. A miniature railway around the lake was added in 1953 and several years later chairlifts were made an appearance.

Visitors to the camp ate in one of four dining halls named after famous Dukes: York; Windsor; Kent and Gloucester. The campers were fed four meals a day including a cooked breakfast, lunch, an afternoon tea of jam and bread plus cakes which was followed later in the evening by a three course dinner.

A typical afternoon's entertainment during mid 1950s featured 'Miss Venus and Tarzan' competitions such as Glamorous Grandmothers and Knobbly Knees as well as Old Time Dancing, Whist Drives and Rambles Over the Headland. Children had a separate

Butlin's Filey – it opened immediately after the end of the war bringing affordable holidays to many.

A Knobbly Knees competition, a staple of any Butlins holiday in the 1950s.

full programme of events including talent competitions, sports of all kinds and shows. They even had their own club 'The Beavers' with its own set of rules:

> **B**e kind to dumb animals
> **E**ager always to help others
> **A**im to be clean, neat and tidy
> **V**ictory by fair play
> **E**nergetic at work and play
> **R**espect for parents and all elders
> And in all things **BE AS EAGER AS A BEAVER**

Evenings were given over to dancing in two separate ballrooms, the Viennese and the Regency, whilst plays and shows were performed in the Gaiety and Empire Theatres. The camp was broken down into houses (as in a school) and frequent inter-house competitions were held. The prize for the happiest married couple competition was a romantic 'Vactric Vacuum Cleaner'. The entertainment finished for the day at a quarter to midnight. 'Good night, Campers, I can see you yawning, Good night, Campers, see you in the morning'.

After the deprivations of wartime, people were looking for any opportunity to enjoy themselves again; Butlin's gave them that chance, at a price they could afford. Once there, food, entertainments, amusements and competitions were all included and whilst the regimentation and crowds of people were not to everyone's taste, it allowed many thousands to take their first holiday in years.

The hotel proprietors, landladies, entrepreneurs and showmen had a boom time in the decade following the end of the war. By the time the 1960s rolled in, times were changing and the writing was on the wall for Yorkshire's seaside resorts.

When charter airline Euravia's Lockheed Constellation took to the skies from Manchester's Ringway Airport on 5 May 1962 bound for Palma via Perpignan, it was opening the door to holidays in the Mediterranean sun for millions of passengers living in the north of England. Many of these would have previously been the life blood of Yorkshire's seaside resorts. From 1960-70, the number of foreign holidays taken increased from four to seven million. By the millennium this had risen to over forty-five million holiday visits.

An increase in car ownership also allowed far more freedom to travel to previously out of the way places. Scarborough, Bridlington and the east coast were no longer an automatic choice. Holidays in Cornwall, Devon or in the countryside of Wales or Scotland became increasingly popular, with visitors often choosing to tour around an area as opposed to spending a week or a fortnight in one spot. The increase in the number of cars on narrow roads and through busy towns led to bottlenecks on the major routes to the coast at Tadcaster and Malton.

The railways were badly hit and by mid 1960s, Bridlington had lost its direct link to the industrial and urban centres of West and South Yorkshire. Scarborough, too, lost rail lines, with its link to Whitby closing in 1965, the picturesque service from Whitby to Loftus having already closed in 1958. Passenger trains through Hornsea and Withernsea ceased in 1964. It had been the railways that had brought hope and ambition to

A 1960s advertisement for Scarborough's top hotels. Shortly after times were going to become much harder.

the east coast towns. Now it had been taken away in what were a series of savage cuts, with little thought to the longer term.

Whilst disposable incomes were rising, the numbers taking a week or fortnight's traditional holiday were falling significantly. There was an increase in day visitors and those seeking cheap and cheerful accommodation. People wanted fewer restrictions and to be free from what were often seen as the petty rules imposed by seaside landladies. A lack of access to their rooms at any time and just as importantly with whom they liked, were major grievances. By the late 1960s, Scarborough alone had over 1,500 flats and flatlets, Bridlington 150, most of which had previously been part of hotels and boarding houses. In 1966, a new hotel was built on the North Bay of Scarborough, the New Scalby Mills. Constructed at a time when other hotels were closing, it never achieved its potential and was demolished in 1988. One of Scarborough's landmark buildings, the Pavilion Hotel, situated opposite the railway station met the same fate in 1973. Bridlington's Alexandra Hotel closed two years later.

Up and down the coast, caravan breaks were big business, either in static caravans or in visitors' own tourers. From Filey down to Spurn Point, caravan parks began to dominate the coast, often being built to within a few feet of the sea, a development that was to cause untold problems within a few years as coastal erosion became more and more of a concern.

Erosion is one of the biggest dangers facing the east coast

CHANGING TIMES

Self-catering bungalows and chalets were cheap and popular but did not always have the facilities imagined:

'Two wooden chalets were rented for the week to house both families. They were on Collins Camp at Filey and ours was named Red Roofs, There was no electricity, gas lights and cooking were via a Calor Gas cylinder which usually ran out just after you arrived. The toilet was outside in a cubicle and was an "Elsan Chemical" unit. No flush facilities, so in hot weather it could get a bit high! To combat the aroma a man came round the site on Sunday morning with a horse and open backed cart and simply tipped the contents of "The Elsan" into the cart then on his way to the next chalet.

'We spent days on the beach happily swimming and playing in the sea whilst Mum sheltered behind a hired wind break sat in a hired deck chair. Food time, and a great tray with mugs and the best cuppa from the beachside café, proper mugs no plastic or cardboard then. We also rented a changing tent, Green canvas on a wooden base about 3 foot square and 6 foot 6ins, high dragged to where you wanted it by the attendant.'

Families loved the cheap and cheerful holidays spent in the holiday parks as Linda Cory fondly remembers:

'I recall many times as a child going to the east coast. The family went to Golden Sands at Withernsea several times. We stayed in a wooden chalet type and I have some vivid memories from those holidays. The chalet had 2 bedrooms, mum and dad in one and me and my sister Carole in the other. They led off a central space which was both living space and dining. There was a small kitchen up the 2 wooden stairs into the front of the chalet. There were swings and slides on the site which we spent hours on. I used to take bread wrapping paper - the old fashioned waxed sort and slide down the slide a few times on it to shine it up. It was quite funny to watch the children sliding off the end of the

Filey beach with its famous changing tents.

slide at a rate of knots because it became so slippery. Probably
a bit dangerous now I think about it!

'For a couple of years there were a lot of children with
thalidomide limbs. It was a very recent thing at the time and the
first time I had seen such children. They were amazing though
and slid down the slide with everyone else.

'There must have been a clubhouse or something on the site
too as I went regularly with dad to play on the penny machines.
One machine was a playing cards one, and the lights lit up in
front of you. You had to put your penny in (old pennies of course
1d) and guess which playing card would be highlighted. My dad
worked out the sequence and we won every time often emptying
the machine. We were caught out eventually and they put "out
of order" on the machine!'

Many holidaymakers were content to stay on the beach near their
caravans and chalets. Food was brought from home and little was spent

on entertainment and recreation. Confidence on the Yorkshire coast was at an all-time low and consequently, attractions began to close, or were inadequately maintained. By 1966, Scarborough only had one surviving cinema, the Odeon, the others mainly succumbing to the growing popularity of the bingo hall. Whitby at one time had four cinemas, only one of which now remains, in the restored Coliseum complex, whilst Bridlington lost the Lounge, the Roxy and the Regal in quick succession.

If cinemas were becoming bingo halls, then other buildings were falling victim to garish, neon-lit amusement arcades including Scarborough Foreshore's old Marine Baths and the former Olympia Exhibition Hall. It was probably a blessing when the Olympia and surrounding buildings were burned to the ground in 1975. The Floral Hall, former home of the famed Fol-de-Rols concert party, closed in 1987. Over the past twenty years it had welcomed well known TV acts such as Les Dawson, Harry Worth, Frank Ifield and Freddie Starr. The public's taste in entertainment was changing though and audiences for this type of variety show were falling rapidly. The hall was replaced by a bowling centre.

Back in the 1960s, the Futurist Theatre under its owner impresario Robert Luff, had played host to some of the biggest names in the rock and pop world as well as successful summer seasons and one off shows. The Beatles played twice, the first concert on 11 December 1963 followed by one in August the following year. Other big acts attracted to the Futurist included The Rolling Stones, The Hollies, Dusty Springfield and The Kinks. Morecambe and Wise and Shirley Bassey also graced its stage. The theatre was expanded in 1968, to cater for expanding audiences, taking over the next-door site of the former Palladium Picture House. It was the end of the last connection to Catlin's renowned Arcadia Theatre. With the new design, the theatre became the fifth largest outside of London. For a while, people flocked to the theatre as it continued to attract big names such as Cilla Black and Jimmy Tarbuck and was the regular home of the Black and White Minstrels up until the 1970s. Sadly, the Futurist too then began to struggle with falling audiences not paying for its upkeep. The theatre

The bright lights of Scarborough's Foreshore today. Not to everyone's taste, but popular nonetheless!

was eventually bought by the council in 1985 for £320,000. Despite pouring in vast amounts of money on renovation, the venue continued to run at a significant loss.

Throughout this period, the town lost many of its theatres and entertainment venues. Probably the saddest was when Gala Land was demolished in 1968. Built as Scarborough Aquarium, it represented all the Victorian dreams of the town. It had become dark, damp and depressing. Somehow appropriately, it became an underground car park that nobody really wanted.

Scarborough had entered the second half of the twentieth century with an array of fading attractions from its Victorian and Edwardian heyday. These, together with its acres of parks and gardens, were costly to maintain and became a constant drain on the council's finances. The Spa complex exemplified this dilemma. With no major work having been undertaken on the site since before World War Two, it was in need of significant refurbishment. After many, sometimes

168

bitter, deliberations, the restoration of the Grand Hall, Ballroom and other areas was completed in 1981 at a cost of over £5 million. Whilst the improvements were not the panacea that had been hoped for, the Spa survived several financial crises that had threated both its theatre and orchestra yet now remains a major part of Scarborough's future.

On the North Bay, attractions such as Watersplash World came and went. One of the most successful was the children's activity park Kinderland. With neither a slot machine nor amusement arcade in sight, visitors for a £2 entry fee had unlimited use of slides, climbing frames, a pedal car track, clock tower, water chute, boating lake and much more. Once again, the well-loved amenity was closed in 2007.

Bridlington like Scarborough was keen to move with the times and the 1960s and '70s saw The Who, Rolling Stones and Status Quo play at the Spa, whilst smaller acts featured at the Grand Pavilion. Summer entertainment at the spa, such as the 1973 Holiday Startime, starring Duggie Chapman, offering an evening of 'Gaiety, Glamour, Comedy and Variety' catered for the older visitor and families.

The Pavilion was eventually transformed into the 3B's Theatre Bar and Restaurant which opened on 25 May 1973, starring TV Comedian Mike Donohoe, before becoming part of the new Leisure World complex in 1987, which was centred around a large indoor tropically-styled swimming pool, complete with water slides. The Floral Pavilion was not as fortunate. After closing, it was allowed to deteriorate before being developed into a bar and restaurant. A low point for the town must have been the loss of the Prince's Parade to a fun fair.

Filey appeared to be bucking the trend when in 1961 a decision was made to build a concert hall in the Crescent Gardens. The existing colonnade was retained but not the bandstand. The new hall was first called the Winter Gardens but eventually changed its name to the Sun Lounge. Filey had always been a quieter and more natural resort and as such was not as susceptible to variations in taste and fashion. The town was not to prove totally immune to the changes in visitor habits, however.

Guest numbers at nearby Butlin's had fallen significantly in the late 1970s and by the end of the decade the north side of the camp was virtually unused and neglected. The Windsor Dining room was abandoned with many of the windows cracked and broken. The camp's own railway station closed in 1977 as the vast majority of visitors now arrived in their own vehicles. It was still a massive shock nevertheless, when towards the end of the 1983 season, Butlin's announced that the Filey camp along with Clacton was to close at the end of the season. It was a major blow not only to the Filey employees, many from outlying villages, who had been planning the 1984 season, but also to the local council who were losing some £350,000 in rates.

The site was immediately put up for sale and sold to Trevor Guy, whose first action was to sell forty acres to the next-door Primrose Valley Caravan Park, a sign of things to come. After a complete refurbishment, the new holiday centre, Amtree Park, was opened with a great fanfare on 24 May 1986. It closed just six weeks later. The camp was demolished over the period 1989-1991. It was not until 2007 that the site was reused, when the luxury Bay Holiday Village was opened.

Of the larger resorts, Whitby, had attracted visitors as keen to soak up its history, the old town and its art and culture as its fine sandy beaches. The arrival in the town in 1997 of HMS *Bark Endeavour*, a scale replica of its eighteenth century namesake boosted the interest in Whitby's maritime heritage, and the local economy, to the tune of £5 million. A further visit several years later was worth even more than that. Coupled with the rise of interest in the resort's 'gothic' connections and the start of the Whitby Goth Weekends, a festival of music and culture, the town has flourished at a time when others have struggled.

The thirty years leading up to the millennium were a very difficult time for Yorkshire's seaside resorts. At the start of the twentyfirst century they were left with difficult decisions about the direction they were to follow.

Renaissance

Yorkshire's seaside resorts faced the new millennium with the future looking bleak. A *Which* report in 1999, claimed that 'the annual exodus to the nearest kiss-me-quick resort has rather gone the way of one piece bathing suits for men, afternoon tea dances and knotted hankies'. Even the county's own tourist board was not beyond criticising the standard of accommodation and the lack of friendliness and hospitality of those running the resorts guesthouses and small hotels.

The two major resorts of Scarborough and Bridlington had lost their attraction to the young and even to a large extent, families. Town centres were rundown and the resorts lacked the facilities that modern visitors demanded. Visitors began to care less about amusement arcades and flashy entertainment venues. Attractions that at one time could only have been found at the coast were now readily available close to home. People cared more about the cleanliness of streets, beaches and seas, walks on unspoilt coastlines, history and culture and good accommodation and food.

It was an indisputable fact that millions of people jetted off around the world for their main holidays. There was a growing realisation that Britain offered some of the most varied and dramatic coastlines in Europe. Television programmes such as *Coast* or others enticing homebuyers to move to the sea highlighted its charms. People did still love the seaside but in different ways. It was up to local councils and private enterprise to fulfil their dreams, albeit at a time of severe financial difficulties.

After winning the English Tourist Board sponsored 'Resorts 2000' competition, there was optimism in the air at Bridlington. In 1998, the town opened its completely renovated South Bay Promenade, the North Bay Promenade having been upgraded some years earlier. Running southwards from the Spa Buildings, the three original promenades were redesigned and refurbished and are now united into one on the seaward side for most of their length. New structures were created along the promenade, including a viewing terrace with shops below, public conveniences and beach huts, culminating in a new stylishly designed café and jetty sculpture on the headland at the Promenade's farthest point, with more new beach huts beyond. Other new facilities included a paddling pool, and a water channel running south to a water wall alongside other original artworks.

The council also attended to its longest outstanding project; the Spa. By 2005, the building was in a terrible condition and a decision was taken to undertake a full and thorough refurbishment of the entire complex. After closing between 2006–2008 it began to attract 'big' names from the world of entertainment and is now a major venue for shows, concerts and conferences. In 2014, blue plaques were installed for Herman Darewski, composer and conductor of light music and for Wallace Hartley, leader of the orchestra playing as the *Titanic* sank. Hartley led an orchestra in the town in 1902.

In May 2016, the town unveiled its new leisure centre built on the site of the previous 'Leisure World'. Planning permission was also given for the construction of a new eighty bed hotel on a nearby site. A possible new Travelodge is also under consideration. Bridlington has also begun to emphasise the attraction of its 'Old Town' with its historic priory, gate and streets of independent shops and restaurants. The filming of the *Dad's Army* movie in the location brought the area to the public's attention.

In order to attract more affluent visitors and encourage them to stay for a weekend or longer, the town needs to provide a wider range of shops, accommodation and restaurants. A regeneration plan is being implemented and there are hopes that the long-awaited Marina may now become a possibility. Bridlington appears to be moving in the right direction.

Scarborough, over the last few years, faced similar challenges to its neighbour. One of the first moves to try and address them was in 2007, when the old Corner Café complex was demolished and replaced by the Sands, a development of luxury apartments spread over two low-rise blocks. The work formed part of a much wider regeneration

Bridlington Spa theatre beautifully restored in 2008.

plan for the North Bay which also included the reopening of the town's Open Air Theatre. Closed in 1986, the once popular attraction was given a major refurbishment and was opened by the Queen on 20 May 2010. Since that date, the venue has hosted some of the biggest names in the music world including Elton John, Status Quo, Jessie J and McFly. A further piece in the jigsaw was the building of the Alpamare Water Park which opened in 2016. Further work needs to be undertaken on the site of the old Atlantis Water Park. Whilst much of the work has been controversial and has angered civic and environmental bodies, it would appear to be paying dividends.

Over on the South Bay, almost £8 million was spent on the renovation of the Spa. One of the areas giving the most concern in Scarborough was the Futurist Theatre on the Foreshore. The vast auditorium, in desperate need of substantial restoration, was the subject of often angry debate. In January 2017, the council voted to demolish the building and redevelop the land. Throughout this turbulent period, one building has stood out in Scarborough and that is the Stephen Joseph Theatre. Now situated in the old Odeon Cinema, it has long been the home of the acclaimed playwright Alan Ayckbourn. Sell out performances continuing to prove that in the twenty-first century, high quality entertainment will still attract visitors.

Of the other resorts under the Borough Council's control, Filey and Whitby appear to have weathered the storm somewhat more easily than the larger towns by concentrating on what they have always offered. Filey a 'traditional seaside resort with a low-key atmosphere offering restful 'get away from it all' holidays,' and Whitby, where visitors are just as likely 'to be sightseeing or hiking as participating in traditional seaside activities'.

Figures for the period 2013-2015, showed that the Scarborough Borough area, incorporating the resorts of Scarborough, Filey and Whitby, together with the villages of Robin Hoods Bay and Staithes, was the second most popular area for British visitors after London, for both holiday trips and holiday spend. Grounds for optimism, most definitely, yes.

Whilst the small towns of Redcar, Saltburn, Hornsea and Withernsea will never return to their dream days, when they had hopes of rivalling Scarborough as a pre-eminent watering place, they continue to offer a getaway for the people of the north east and

The former small fishing villages of Robin Hoods Bay and Staithes continue to draw visitors looking for more than just a beach. (Adobe Images)

Humberside, the beach, the sea and the fresh air being the main ingredients. In the south of the region, erosion is shrinking the coastline by up to two metres per year, one of the fastest rates in the world, threatening people's homes and holiday retreats. Not a new problem, but one that needs to be addressed.

Throughout their history, Yorkshire's seaside resorts have had to adapt to meet the constantly changing requirements of their visitors and there is nothing to suggest that this will change in the future. Some things remain constant, however, and that is the love of the county's coast from generation to generation and that is the resorts greatest hope for the future.

'This year we took our new campervan to Bridlington and to Filey. Both times with our granddaughter, little Abbie. It's great how you never fall out of love with the east coast and even greater to see your family finding the same love of the seaside. We crabbed, and built sand pies and ate ice cream. We also wrapped up against the fierce wind and rain and walked and drank warm coffee to thaw out.

'So many people love the east coast it must have some magic to it.'

Bibliography

Anonymous, *A Journey from London to Scarborough in Several Letters From a Gentleman There, to His Friend in London* (Ward and Chandler, London 1733)

BAKER, Edward, *Sojourn in Scarborough – The Diary of Edward Baker,* The Old Hall Press, Leeds, 1984.

BEBB, Prudence, *Life in Regency Scarborough,* William Sessions, York, 1997.

BERRY, Kevin, *Charlotte Brontë at the Seaside,* Highgate Publishing, Beverley, 1990.

BINNS, Dr Jack, *The History of Scarborough, North Yorkshire,* Blackthorne Press, Pickering, 2003.

BROADRICK, G., *A New Scarborough Guide,* Scarborough 1806; 1810; 1811.

CAULFIELD, James, *Portraits, Memoirs and Characters of Remarkable Persons from the Revolution in 1688 to the End of the Reign on George II,* 1819.

CHAPMAN, Mave and Ben, *Pierrots of the Yorkshire Coast,* Hutton Press, Beverley, 1988.

DEFOE, Daniel, *A Tour thro' the Whole Island of Great Britain,* 1724-1727.

FEARON, Michael, The *History of Filey, North Yorkshire,* Blackthorne Press, Pickering, 2008.

FEARON, Michael, *From Fishing Village to Edwardian Resort*, Hutton Press, Beverley, 1990.

FELTHAM, John, *A Guide to all the Watering and Sea-Bathing Places*, Longman, Hirst, Rees, Orme and Brown, London, 1813; 1815.

FIENNES, Celia, *Through England on a Side Saddle in the Time of William and Mary*, The Leadenhall Press, London, 1888

FURBY, J., *Picturesque Excursions from Bridlington Quay*, Furby, Bridlington 1841.

GRANVILLE, Augustus Bozzi, *The Spas of England and Principal Sea-Bathing Places*, Henry Colburn, London, 1841.

BIBLIOGRAPHY

HARRISON, Stephen, *The History of Hornsea: From the Earliest Times to the Year 2000*, Blackthorne Press, Pickering, 2006.

HINDERWELL, Thomas, *The History and Antiquities of Scarborough*, York, 1798; 1811; 1832.

HITCHES, Mike, *Filey Through Time*, Amberley Publishing, Stroud, 2011.

HUTTON, W., *The Scarborough Tour in 1803*, John Nichols and Sons, London, 1804.

NEAVE, David, *Port, Resort and Market Town*, Hull Academic Press, Hull, 2000.

NEAVE, David and Susan, *Bridlington, An Introduction to its History and Buildings*, Smith Settle, Otley, 2000.

PEARSON, Trevor, *Scarborough, A History*, Phillimore, Chichester, 2009.

PONTEFRACT, E. and **HARTLEY,** M., *Yorkshire Tour,,* J, M Dent, London 1939.

ROWNTREE, Arthur (ed.), *The History of Scarborough*, J.M. Dent, London, 1931.

SMOLLETT, Tobias, *The Expedition of Humphrey Clinker*, London, 1771.

THEAKSTON, S. W., *Guide to Scarborough*, Theakston, Scarborough, 1840; 1854; 1860.

THOMPSON, J., *Historical Sketches of Bridlington*, Thompson, Bridlington, 1821.

TWEDDELL, George Markham, Visitor's *Hand-Book to Redcar, Coatham, and Saltburn-By-The-Sea,* Webster, Redcar, 1863.

WHITE, AAndrew, *A History of Whitby*, Phillimore, Bognor Regis, 1993.

WHITTAKER, Meredith, *The Book of Scarborough Spaw,* Barracuda Books, Buckingham, 1984.

WHITE, W., *A Month in Yorkshire*, Chapman and Hall, London, 1858.

WHITE, W., *History, Gazetteer and Directory of the East and North Ridings of Yorkshire*, White, Sheffield 1840.

WILKINSON, Colin, *Whitby Between the Wars*, Amberley Publishing, Stroud, 2016.

YOUNG, Rev. G., *A Picture of Whitby and its Environs*, Rodgers, Whitby 1824.

Guide Books, Brochures and seaside ephemera have also been an extremely useful source of information as was the modern-day blessing/curse of the internet.

Index

178

INDEX